The Hipster Librarian's Guide to Teen Craft Projects

Tina Coleman
and Peggie Llanes

Foreword by Heather Booth

American Library Association
Chicago 2009

Tina Coleman is a member specialist for the Member Development department of the American Library Association. As marketing coordinator for ALA Editions and ALA Graphics, she won the 2006 Staff Achievement Award. Her work in marketing for different areas of the ALA has allowed her to use her creative talents and develop a working knowledge of the library world. As a crafter Tina has built an artistic ethic that concentrates on recycling, deconstructing, and promoting the idea that everyone can be creative. She and her coauthor/mother, Peggie Llanes, also give workshops on how to build a craft program in the library.

Peggie Llanes worked in various capacities at the Christopher House day care/social services center in Chicago, including as director of the after-school program. During this time she had extensive training in child development, social service, and community and group work, which tapped into her desire to craft and be creative on the job and at home. Through her experience working with underprivileged children, she developed a keen sense of the importance of presenting open-ended projects that would promote creativity and individuality and enhance self-esteem under a tight budget.

The paper used in this publication meets the minimum requirements of American National Standard for Information Sciences—Permanence of Paper for Printed Library Materials, ANSI Z39.48-1992. ∞

Library of Congress Cataloging-in-Publication Data
Coleman, Tina.
The hipster librarian's guide to teen craft projects / Tina Coleman and Peggie Llanes ; foreword by Heather Booth.
p. cm.
ISBN 978-0-8389-0971-3 (alk. paper)
1. Young adults' libraries—Activity programs. 2. Libraries and teenagers. 3. Handicraft.
I. Llanes, Peggie. II. Title.

Z718.5.C62 2009
027.62′6—dc22 2008019988

ISBN-13: 978-0-8389-0971-3

Printed in the United States of America
13 12 11 10 09 5 4 3 2 1

Foreword, by Heather Booth v
Acknowledgments vii
Introduction 1

Project 1 **Creative Marbles 7**
Project 2 **Melted Crayon Bookmarks 11**
Project 3 **Pressed Flower Note Cards 17**
Project 4 **Blank Books 23**
Project 5 **Layered Fabric Collages 31**
Project 6 **Coasters and Trivets 37**
Project 7 **Rubber Band Bracelets and Necklaces 43**
Project 8 **Mosaic Tile Jewelry 49**
Project 9 **Woven Paper Baskets 57**
Project 10 **Vinyl Totes 65**
Project 11 **T-shirt Reconstruction 73**
Project 12 **Book Pillows 81**

Appendix: Supplies, Tools, and Project Materials 85
Glossary 87
Resources 91

WEB Printable one-page instruction sheets for each program are available on the book's website: www.ala.org/editions/extras/Coleman09713.

Foreword

GATHER A GROUP of YA librarians together and inevitably the conversation turns to programming.

First the questions: "Do you do teen programming? How is your turnout? Do you have a budget for it?"

And then the frustration: "Now that the community center has open gym night, we've lost our core group. I spent hours preparing and only two kids showed up! The presenter was great, but he cost half my summer budget."

Which all comes down to the big issue: "I just don't know what they want!"

Teens don't just want to *see,* they want to *do.*

What teens want is to be active agents in their own lives, to be treated like the adults they are striving to become, and to have their views and interests respected. When a library presents teens with the opportunity to have these things, it has the underpinnings of a successful teen program.

With sports, speech club, musicals, SAT prep, Scouting, jobs, chores, homework, band practice, and more competing with the library for teens' after-school time—not to mention just hanging out with friends in person or online—the library needs to offer teens something unique and valuable in its programming, too. Teens want something they can't get elsewhere, something that they can become personally involved in, not just as passive viewers but as active participants. With the push in YA library programming moving from programming *for* teens to programming *with* teens, *The Hipster Librarian's Guide to Teen Craft Projects* provides librarians creative ideas for rising to this challenge. Not only are the crafts presented visually interesting and developmentally appropriate for teen and adult participants, many can be couched within a larger project of teens being of service to others in their community, be it the Friends of the Library, seniors groups, or preschooler storytime attendees.

Crafting is a logical programming choice for teens as it provides an opportunity to be actively involved in creating something personal and appeals to the burgeoning adolescent interest in self-expression. Plus, in recent years, crafting has become hip again. Teens and young adults are gathering in coffeehouses and homes to knit, create one-of-a-kind T-shirts, fashion manga-inspired stuffed toys, and more. These projects are appropriately a generation away from the cut-and-paste crafts useful in children's programming in that they provide the crafter with a basic format and then allow unlimited creativity

Vinyl Totes, on page 65

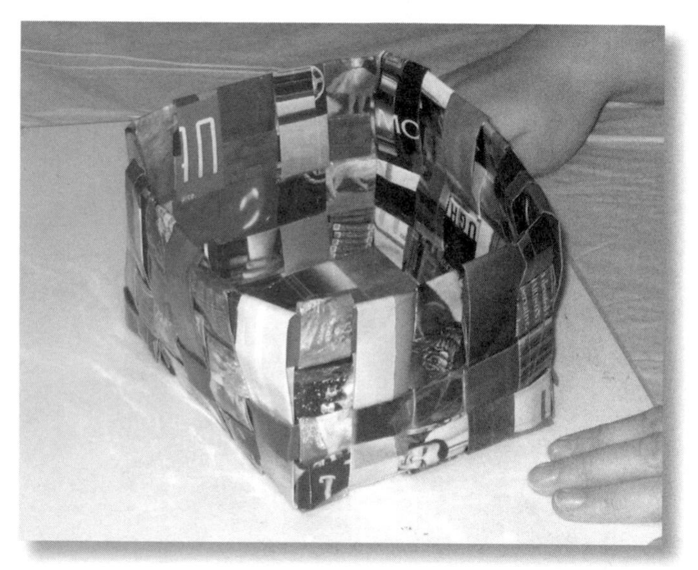

Woven paper basket, on page 57

in executing the project. The jewelry projects (chapters 7 and 8) provide a teen the opportunity to create something that she feels is stylish and represents herself, and then to wear it—prominently displaying that self-expression and her own creativity. Creative Marbles (chapter 1) are an ideal way for teens to easily make a visual statement that can be displayed on refrigerators or lockers. Layered Fabric Collages (chapter 5) provide the vehicle for a wide range of self-expression depending on the angle that the librarian facilitators promote and the teen participants pursue. Blank Books (chapter 4) take the idea of self-expression even further, first helping participants create beautiful and meaningful books and then providing them a space to write or sketch their thoughts and ideas.

That most of the projects can be done mainly with repurposed and recycled materials is not only a boon to the environment and librarians with more time than money for programming but also an appealing draw for many teens as they are becoming increasingly aware of their place in the world around them. The sense of justice and social responsibility is strong in the teen years. Library programs can encourage such responsibility with environmentally aware projects such as Pressed Flower Note Cards (chapter 3), projects using primarily repurposed materials such as Melted Crayon Bookmarks (chapter 2) and Woven Paper Baskets (chapter 9), and even by asking teens to delve into their own closets for T-shirt Reconstruction (chapter 11). Additionally, with an eye to social involvement, the authors' suggested uses for many of the projects include working with shut-ins, younger children, or Friends of the Library groups—all positive ways for socially aware teens to engage with others in their community.

If you have been hesitant to try programming for teens, or if past programs have been less than enthusiastically received, I would encourage you to try one of these craft projects. Make a few examples to display in a window or on a counter to promote the program and have at it! The relatively low cost and the ability to use things you likely already have around the library make many of these ideas feasible even on a meager budget, and the time it takes to create the examples is just about all the time it takes to prepare for many of the programs. If you already have a teen group, you could enlist them in creating samples for you, and in doing so test out the process—and garner their interest at the same time! Have fun with the projects, have fun with the teens, and keep in mind that what teens want most—respect and the opportunity to be themselves—is something that every librarian already has the ability to provide, cost-free.

—Heather Booth

Acknowledgments

Thanks to my dad, who served the cause of this book with culinary expertise, supply runs, and an uncanny ability to measure a straight line, and to Mel, Terra, Cody, Dylan, and the rest of the munchkins for playing guinea pig every time we needed them to. Thanks to Heather Booth for her library-side view of every project, and to Jenni, Christine, Catherine, and the entire ALA Editions team, who not only helped with editorial questions but also suffered through endless show-and-tell sessions. Most of all, thanks to my mom, for coming on the adventure of writing this book, for every midnight session of figuring out which glue works best, for grumbling along every time a stitch wasn't perfect, and for giving me the creative practicality I have in the first place. And thanks to Pat.

—Tina Coleman

First I will have to thank Tina for inviting me to take part in this adventure. It has been fun, exciting, and sometimes exhausting working with her. I am very proud that she asked me to join her. We always inspire each other! Along the way we have learned to be good partners.

I also thank my husband, Ray, for his endless support. He has been our biggest fan!

Thanks also to Melissa, my special-needs daughter, for being on her very best behavior and for showing us that she, too, could do many of these projects.

And thanks to the rest of my family who endured our endless talk about crafting projects and never once showed their boredom but offered us encouragement.

—Peggie Llanes

Introduction

Crafting? For Teens? Seriously?

At a time when teens are happily "plugged in" to video games, iPods, the Internet, texting, and any other techno-gadget you can think of, can something like crafting really be put into the context of their lives? *Yes!*

These days crafting is not your grandmother's notion of crocheting tea cozies and tatting doilies. And it's not the kindergarten tradition of paper plates and library paste. Crafting is neither a boring time-waster nor a baby game. Crafting can be a hip-and-happening, cutting-edge, Do-It-Yourself way of life. It's cool. Geek-chic. And with the help of our book, you can make this particular brand of cool readily available at your library. Although the projects we've included draw on basic techniques, we've put a hip spin on them. Things like collaging, decoupage, or pressing flowers are hardly new ideas, even to teens, but adding twists on materials or uses revamps these age-old techniques.

If you look around, you can find crafters of every stripe in almost every nook and cranny. Traditional crafts, like quilting and knitting, have dedicated practitioners who meet regularly, not just making your usual set of afghans and booties but knocking out Hogwarts scarves and quilts with punky patterns. T-shirt reconstruction has become high fashion, with celebrities sporting the shirts in movies and on TV. Whole communities exist on the Internet just so crafters around the world can trade ideas and show off results. Television shows like *Project Runway* and *Trading Spaces* have built up the DIY attitude in adults and teens alike. With the project ideas presented here and a good supply of project materials relevant for teens (e.g., graphic novel scraps, fabrics with cool patterns, creative embellishments), you can offer a crafting program that truly reflects today's teen culture and interests.

T-shirt reconstruction, on page 73

And Just Where Does Crafting Fit into My Library's Mission?

Teens are at an age of discovering who they are and establishing their own identity amid the pressure of remaining cool to their friends. Crafting can provide an outlet for them to express their individuality and gain confidence. It can help develop creative thinking in teens who may not think they are creative.

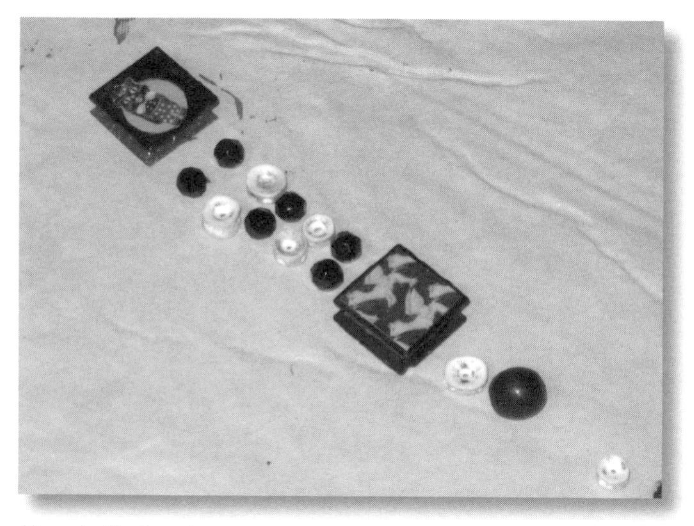
Mosaic tile jewelry, on page 49

Most of all, crafting can help kids think outside the box. Libraries and teen programs already tend to draw the loners and kids who feel like outsiders. A good crafting program or a teen program that builds crafting into its regular activities can show teens that they aren't as isolated or different as they fear they are, and it can help them to be proud of the differences that they do have.

Crafting can also help teens in more practical ways. The skills they can learn with crafting can be applied to other areas of life, and of course vice versa. Problem solving, patience, teamwork, and self-sufficiency are all skills that can be learned and reinforced through crafting. It can give a focus for discussion and ideas. Crafting is an open and versatile art form, and that alone will appeal to young people. In crafting there is no right way or wrong way to do things, just different approaches to the project for unique results. With teen culture so adept at promoting conformity, crafting can provide an avenue for a stronger self-image and show that other options are available.

A craft program can bring benefits to the library itself. If you already have a regular teen group, crafting can offer fun activities and may lure some new kids in through friends and word of mouth. A display of the great project results can be fabulous advertising for your craft program. The crafts we present here can also be used as good jumping-off points for research into other arts or techniques. Basket weaving, bookbinding, sewing, jewelry making—these are all legitimate art forms with long histories and almost endless techniques. If teens learn the basics through these projects at the library, they are conveniently in the perfect place to go further and learn more.

Adding craft projects is also a good way to enhance existing programs. In the introduction to each project we offer some suggestions about how it may fit in with different types of programs. Summer reading, library campaigns, book clubs, and other programs can be expanded to include crafting.

You can use crafting as a great way to build communities. Teen groups are the obvious choice, but you can use craft projects to bring other groups together. If your library has a reading buddy program for teens and younger kids, some of these crafts can be great projects to help build that relationship. They can be used to make gifts for library guests, special visitors, or shut-in patrons, or even for sale or auction as part of a library fund-raiser. Many of these projects are great parent-child activities, providing a fun way to spend quality time. Alternatively, you can encourage groups to form around activities. If you have adult patrons who are crafters, you can pair them up with the teens and start a mentoring program through crafting. If you have knitters, scrapbookers, crocheters, sewers, and the like among your adult patrons, ask if they would be interested in teaching these specialized skills to your teen crafters.

Group crafting is a good way to encourage socializing. Used as an icebreaking activity, it allows context for teamwork as well as general conversation to help participants get to know one another. Even with groups in which everyone already knows one another, craft projects can keep people open to others' ideas or encourage collaboration. It sounds pretty remedial, but sharing is a skill you're never too old to practice, and craft projects offer infinite opportunities to do so.

Of course these projects don't have to be used only with teen groups. Simply changing some of the materials you offer for a project can make it appeal to adults, senior groups, younger kids, or patrons with disabilities. Crafting can also be a great way to increase involvement of any of these groups in your library community. If you have scrapbookers or gardeners or just crafty people, you may encourage them to build a group that uses the library for regular meetings. If you already run a teen crafting group or use crafts regularly as a part of your teen programming, you have a great resource for fresh ideas and/or volunteers.

Okay! I'm Sold! But What about the Costs Involved?

We've established that crafting can be a fun and useful tool in the library. Now the question is this: How do you pay for it? Luckily crafting can be very economical. Of course there are crafting hobbies that require big investment, but generally you don't need to spend a lot of money on supplies, especially at a library. A lot of your resources can be things you already have on hand or can obtain through donations.

Recycling is a running theme in the projects we provide here. The craft projects we offer tend to recycle materials or find new uses for items, partly because the creativity required for repurposing appeals to teens and offers them the opportunity to see objects in different ways, but also because it is a practical solution to budgetary constraints. The world is full of free craft supplies if you use your imagination. Knowing how and where to get materials is the real key. Building your resources can require as much creative thinking as building the crafts themselves. We offer some hints to get you started, but the most important thing is to keep your mind (and your eyes) open.

There are some things you will need to just break down and pay for, but this doesn't mean you need to pay a lot. For the most part, you'll need to buy tools—glue guns, sewing machines or supplies, grommet setters, and the like. In the Supplies and Tools List at the back of the book, we've highlighted the things you'll probably need to purchase.

For tools, the best place to start is the hardware store. There is a lot of crossover now between hardware and craft stores, and usually you can find things cheaper at the hardware store. Glue guns and yardsticks, for example, are much cheaper there. If you can't find something at the hardware store, it's time to move on to a craft supply store, hobby shop, or sewing supply store. Depending on the area you're in, grommet setters, sewing machines and supplies, and certain other tools may only be found at these specialty shops. Keep in mind, too, that the Internet is becoming a better resource for finding things at a good price. If you're really strapped for cash but have time to do some research, this can be a lifesaver.

Although you should try to get as much as possible through salvage and donation, if you do need to buy materials, the best places to look are dollar and discount stores. Craft sticks, white glue, pencils, glue sticks, and even glassware and containers are always readily available at dollar stores.

Discount stores can be a great resource for plain picture frames, clear vinyl shower curtains, fabric, beads, and more.

You can also keep an eye out for deals at thrift shops and garage sales. These can be good resources for any number of items from large picture frames to clothing for fabric scraps. Availability is more challenging, though, so you'll need to be canny. Fabric in particular is easy to find at thrift shops and garage sales. Tablecloths, bedsheets, curtains, and the like are really just large pieces of fabric with hems, and they are all readily available at resale shops. The same is true for costume jewelry and clothing, and most can be had for a few dollars. Just make sure to launder all your fabric items before adding them to your supply.

Recycling tools and materials through donation is another great way to build up your supplies, and it allows your patrons to help with the program. For some projects this can be as simple as asking participants to bring something from home. You can also have a supplies-drive, asking patrons to donate clean clothing, calendars, costume jewelry, and even leftovers from their own craft or home-renovation projects. This can be a good trade-off, allowing patrons to clear some useful things out of their houses and at the same time building up your supplies. As you do this, though, keep in mind the space you have available to store things. If you're in a small library with limited space, you may not have room for all the donations you get.

This of course leads us to what you should save. Beyond the things you've asked your patrons to donate, you also have items specific to the library that may be useful for your crafting programs. This is especially true of paper scrap. Keep some of your old catalogs that have cool pictures or illustrations of book covers. Books and graphic novels that are damaged or need to be taken out of circulation can be used in any number of ways. Magazines, out-of-date maps, and posters are perfect for many of the projects in this book. It's a good rule of thumb to look at anything and everything for its crafty potential before pitching it. Likely as not it can be used for something. Also, make sure to look outside your area of the library. The children's librarian may have some books, catalogs, or even crafting odds and ends that he or she doesn't need.

With some creative thinking and a little extra storage space, you can keep your craft program well stocked for many of these projects. And by looking critically at the requisite supplies and judiciously paring the materials, you should be able to do most of these projects for next to nothing.

Any Last Words of Advice?

Organizing your materials is an important detail that will keep your programs moving smoothly and with fewer headaches. Store like materials together, keeping all your beading supplies in one box, your fabric in another, and so on. It's also useful to sort some of your bulkier supplies further if you can. Keeping paper scrap by theme or type will make it easier to pull only what you want for a specific project later. Fabric should be sorted by color or by weight. Organizing materials can be built into an activity for some of your teen group members as well, and doing so may help them gain a sense of ownership of the program. It may even encourage them to clean up after themselves—if you're lucky.

Tools should be labeled with your library name and address and kept separate from materials when possible. Because they will require the most investment, you may want to keep them away from general access, giving them to teens to use as they need them. Make sure to keep your tools clean and in good repair.

Painted tile for a trivet, on page 37

It is important to stress that whenever you can, you should do the project first before bringing it to your teens. This will give you some experience with the craft and provide you with a finished sample to show the group. This will also prepare you for any questions or give you an idea of what may need some extra attention with your particular group of teens. Any of these projects can be given to crafty teens to do on their own. You could even ask one of them to guest-host a session with his or her own version of the craft as the sample.

At the end of every project, in a section called Adaptations, we've touched on ways to tailor the projects for different groups like seniors, younger kids, or patrons with developmental disabilities. Usually this is just a matter of adjusting the kinds of materials you offer and doing a little more prep work beforehand.

We've also included spin-off ideas that use the same techniques with minor adjustments of measurements or materials. We recommend you do the project as written before attempting spin-offs so you get the techniques well in mind before changing things.

Along with the Supplies and Tools List and the Project Materials List, which have everything that we call for in all the projects, we've included a glossary of techniques and supplies that may be unfamiliar to some. This glossary should help you track down supplies or give you enough information to find a substitute. We've also included a short list of books and websites that may come in handy for ideas or that teens may want to check out to showcase their finished projects.

If you use this book as your teaching copy, we've included an area at the end of each project for you to make notes. We encourage you to write down how a project worked with a group and make notes about what you may need to change for next time. Or if you or the participants get new ideas as you go, jot them down for the next time around.

At the ALA Editions web page associated with this book, www.ala.org/editions/extras/Coleman09713, you'll find single-page instruction sheets that you can print and pass out to group members. And when you've made your way through all the crafts here, check out our ArystoCrafts site (www.arystocrafts.com) for more ideas!

Creative Marbles

Finished creative marbles, with examples of magnet, clutch-pin, and bar-pin backings

Difficulty: Easy
Time: 60 minutes
Supervision: Light
Group Size: 6–8 teens
Mess Factor: Light mess

MARBLE MAGNETS HAVE been all the rage online for a few years, and the project can be easily adapted for library programs with your teens. Because the basic project is so simple—just pictures or words glued to craft marbles—the finished results can fit any type of programming you may need prompts or props for.

For poetry programs, have your teens make marble magnet words to create their own magnetic poetry sets. Or have a whole group make marbles with words and pictures, then invite the participants to draw marbles out of a bag or basket for a poetry slam challenge.

These clever marbles can also be used as storytelling tokens. Once your group makes a bunch of marbles, have them draw from a central pile to build a story together, using the words and pictures on the marbles as prompts. Similarly, have the teens use the tokens as an icebreaker game, telling a story about the image or question on the token.

Teen book groups can use marbles as discussion prompts, using who, what, and where questions or themes in the pictures and words used to make the marbles.

The marbles can be made into great gift pieces like brooches or pins, paperweights, or (of course) magnets. Your teen group or Friends group can also create these as gifts for seniors or homebound patrons. If nothing else, the marbles alone are immensely fun to make and play with!

A printable one-page instruction sheet for this program is available on the book's website: www.ala.org/editions/extras/Coleman09713.

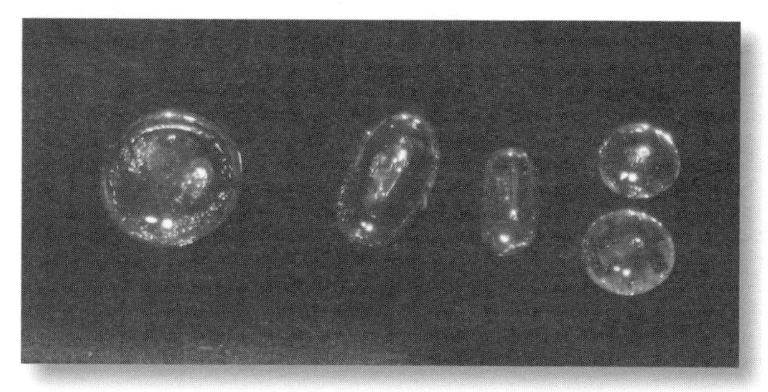

Examples of garden marbles needed for this project

Supplies and Tools

brushes
decoupage medium
hot glue and hot-glue gun (optional) *or* beading/jewelry glue
pencils or pens
small scissors (1 for each participant)
Styrofoam trays

Materials

cork (optional)
craft marbles (these come in various sizes)
felt (optional)
magnets (optional)
paint (optional)
paper scrap
pin backs (optional)

Room Requirements

1 table
extra wastebaskets

Prep Work

Getting the Project Ready

Wipe the marbles to make sure they are free of dust or grime. Choose material from your paper scrap. Choose your paper scrap according to the type of program you're working on (e.g., text sources only, comic books, nature or travel scenes, etc.).

Getting the Room Ready

This project will require a slight break in the middle if you plan to use the marbles to create magnets, pins, or other finished pieces or if you plan to add felt to your tokens. You'll want to set up differently for each segment.

The first segment (steps 1 and 2) will involve cutting out the pictures and words, then using decoupage to glue them onto the marbles. For this stage, place the paper resources in the middle of the table within easy reach of all participants. Each participant should have a supply of marbles, a pair of small scissors, a pencil or pen, and a Styrofoam tray to hold his or her creations. When participants are ready to decoupage the pictures and words onto the marbles, each person should have a small brush, a small container of decoupage medium, and a tray of marbles.

The second segment, finishing the marbles with magnets or pin backs as described in step 3, is optional.

Directions

Step 1: Cutting Your Pictures

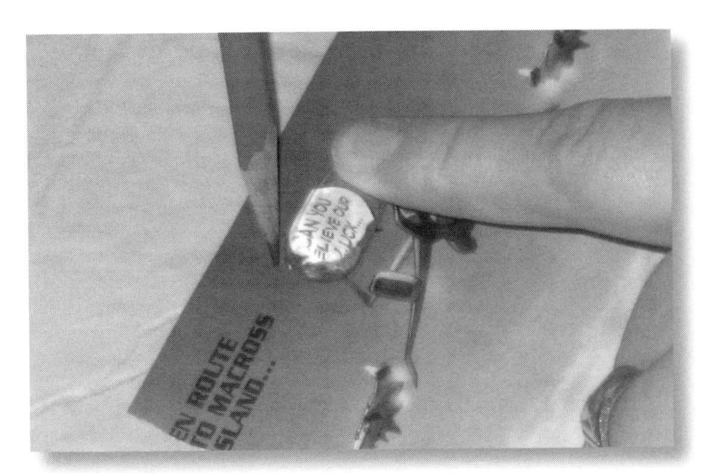

Tracing the image around the marble

Looking through the paper scrap, find words or pictures that will fit the flat side of the marbles. If you're having trouble, leaf through the scrap until you find a page that jumps out at you. Then just pass a blank marble over the page until you find something that works.

Once you've chosen a word or picture, place a marble over the item and trace around it with your pencil. Then lift the marble and use the scissors to cut around the pencil line. If your cutout doesn't match perfectly, don't worry. You can trim it later.

Put your picture under your marble, move it to your tray, and continue looking for more pictures until you have something for each of your marbles.

Here are some design tips:

When using comic books, remember that word balloons can make excellent marbles.

The finished marbles look better when the entire flat surface on the bottom of the marble is taken up by an image.

If you have a cool picture that's too big for your marble, use just a piece of that image.

Sometimes just a pattern or texture will make a great image.

Step 2: Decoupaging

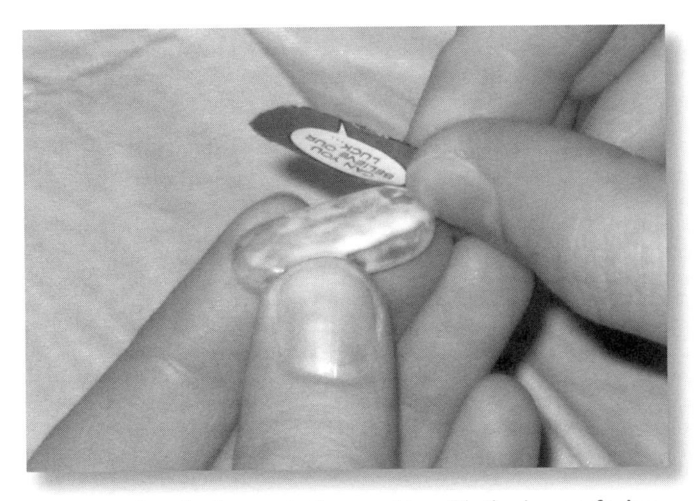

Decoupaging the image to the marble with the image facing into the decoupage medium

This step can get kind of messy, so be prepared to get glue on your hands.

Once you have all your pictures or words cut out, you'll want to have your decoupage medium and brush handy. Brush a light coat of decoupage medium onto the flat surface of the marble. Place the picture *with the side you want showing facing into the decoupage medium.* (It will dry clear, so don't worry.) Press your picture firmly into place, and then brush another light coat of decoupage medium onto the back of the picture. If paper is hanging slightly over the edge of the marble, run your finger around it and press it up around the marble. If you have a lot of overhang, you may want to leave it and trim later.

As you decoupage each marble, place it onto your tray *upside down* to dry. When all your marbles are decoupaged, leave them to dry for at least twenty minutes.

Step 3: Finishing

If you plan to use your marbles as tokens and don't want to add felt to the back, then you are done as soon as your marbles dry. However, even if you just want the marbles to be set out for your teens to play with, they'll last a lot longer and have a more finished appearance if you felt or paint the back.

Before adding whatever backing you've chosen, check each marble and clean up any stray glue spots on the faces or use your scissors to trim away any overhanging edges.

Painting the back of the marbles is the easiest and most straightforward finish. You may want to do this even if you plan to add a pin back or magnet. Color doesn't necessarily matter, but remember that the paint will show through any uncovered places on the back of your marble.

If you're planning to use your marbles as tokens, it's a good idea to felt the back of the marbles so they're less likely to damage tables or other library furniture. Measure the felt the same way you measured the pictures, tracing around the marble with a pencil or pen and cutting on the line. Use hot glue to glue the felt to the back of the marble. This may require more supervision of the group as they use the hot-glue gun. White glue will also work, but because the felt is quite porous, it will take some time to dry completely.

Adding a magnet or pin back is as easy as dabbing a drop of hot glue onto the back of the marble and placing the magnet or pin back in place. Again, using the hot-glue gun may require more direct supervision of your group. Other glues, such as jewelry glue, will work as well. If you prefer not to use a hot-glue gun, check your local craft shop or art supply store for other options.

Spin-offs

Paperweights, game tokens (chess, tic-tac-toe, checkers).

Adaptations

You can adapt this project easily for younger patrons or those with developmental disabilities by using larger craft marbles and having the paper resources cut into more manageable sizes. You may also need to offer more help with cutting and tracing, or have the pictures precut.

Adults or seniors may also have fun with this project, although you may want to adjust your paper resources accordingly or have participants bring in some resources from home.

Notes

Melted Crayon Bookmarks

Difficulty: Easy
Time: 30–60 minutes
Supervision: Medium
Group Size: 6–8 teens (make sure there is enough supervision for ironing)
Mess Factor: Messy

Finished melted crayon bookmarks

MELTING THINGS IS always fun! These creative bookmarks are fun and simple. Building this project is an easy add-on for summer reading programs. Teens can make bookmarks for themselves or as gifts for friends, reading buddies, seniors, or shut-in patrons. Given the abstract nature of the results, this project could work well with programming focusing on art and artists. Adding quotations can also make the project fit in with poetry programming or with a specific book.

Please be aware that depending on the type of crayon you use, crayon color might be transferred to book pages when the bookmarks are in use. To guard against this transfer, you may want to use a spray fixative (use one that is specifically designed for crayon or pastels). Alternatively, and less expensively, you can laminate the finished bookmarks with the packing-tape method used in the Woven Paper Basket project and the Pressed Flower Note Cards project.

A printable one-page instruction sheet for this program is available on the book's website: www.ala.org/editions/extras/Coleman09713.

Supplies and Tools

glue stick (1 for each participant)
hole punch
iron
ironing board (optional)
masking tape
paper plates
parchment or waxed paper
pencil (1 for each participant)
ruler (1 for each participant)
scissors (1 pair for each participant)

Styrofoam trays (large size; 1 for each participant)
towels (2 old ones to use as pressing cloths)
vegetable peelers (1 for each participant)
white glue

Materials

colored card stock or premade blank bookmarks
crayons (the children's librarian may have some leftover stubs that you can scavenge)
embellishments (beads, sequins, etc.; optional)
markers (optional)
tassel materials (cord, embroidery floss, twine, etc.)
vellum quotes (optional)

Room Requirements

2 tables (one for ironing, covered with towels; one covered with newspaper or drop cloth)
extra wastebaskets (including one by the ironing station)

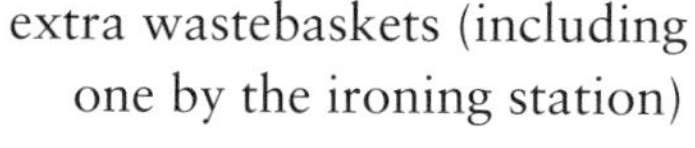

Bookmark blanks folded in half lengthwise

Prep Work

Getting the Project Ready

Precut and fold the card stock into the bookmark blanks (or use ready-made blanks). Dimensions on the final bookmark can vary, but a good rule of thumb is around 7 inches by 3 inches. To get this size, cut the card stock down to 7 inches by 6 inches and fold in half lengthwise.

Getting the Room Ready

The project will run more smoothly if you have each participant's tray of supplies set up on the activity table beforehand. At the main table, each participant should have a vegetable peeler to grate the crayons, a glue stick, a pencil, a ruler, scissors, and a Styrofoam tray to work on and transport the project to and from the ironing station. Place crayons and embellishments in the middle of the table for the group to share. Paper plates should also be available as needed in the middle of the table. Remind participants to use a separate plate for each color of crayon shavings, as the colored shavings will blend.

Create an ironing station separate from the main activity. Keep the iron plugged in but at a low temperature when not in use. Have the waxed paper or parchment paper at this station as well. You may want to have precut sheets of the parchment paper or waxed paper available just to move things along more smoothly once the project starts.

Directions

Step 1: Preparing the Crayons

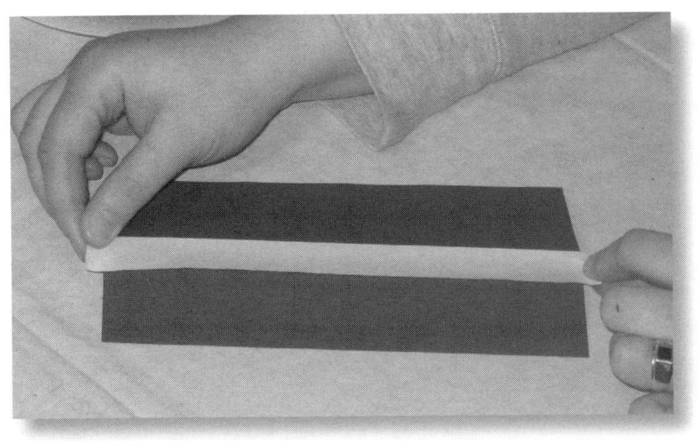
Masking off the back of the bookmark blank by taping along the fold

Using the vegetable peeler, grate crayons onto paper plates. Changing the pressure on the peeler or the length of the stroke will change the consistency of your shavings. Remember to use a different paper plate for each color.

Many varieties of crayons are available now, and different types will yield different results. Try glitter crayons for a subtle sparkle. Artist pastels will melt a bit thicker for a more textured look.

Step 2: Applying the Colors

Place a strip of masking tape along the left side of the fold on the bookmark blank. This will be the back of your bookmark, and you'll want to keep the crayon from getting on this side.

Next, sprinkle crayon shavings onto the front of the bookmark blank. It's better to use less of the crayon shavings than you think you need. You can always add more in a second layer, but if you have too much, you'll just end up with a messy, waxy blob.

Crayon shavings scattered onto the face of the bookmark

The way in which you lay down your colors will give you different results. Sprinkling a lot of different colors on at once will blend the colors when they are ironed, whereas putting down one color, ironing, then putting a different color over that and ironing again will give a more layered effect. Single colors can also give a nice effect, especially on colored card stock.

You can also arrange the pattern of the shavings, but very minimally. It's best not to try for specific shapes when putting down your shavings, but you can create stripes of color or more abstract representations.

Step 3: Ironing

Melted crayon shavings after ironing

Once you have a layer of shavings ready to iron, *carefully* carry your tray over to the ironing station. Place the unfolded bookmark on the ironing board or towel, being careful not to shake off the shavings. Cover the bookmark with a piece of parchment paper or waxed paper, and then cover that with a thin towel or pressing cloth. Set the iron's temperature on high and firmly run the iron over the pressing cloth. *Do not use steam.* Press for about thirty seconds. Lift the pressing cloth to see if the crayon is melted. If not, press again.

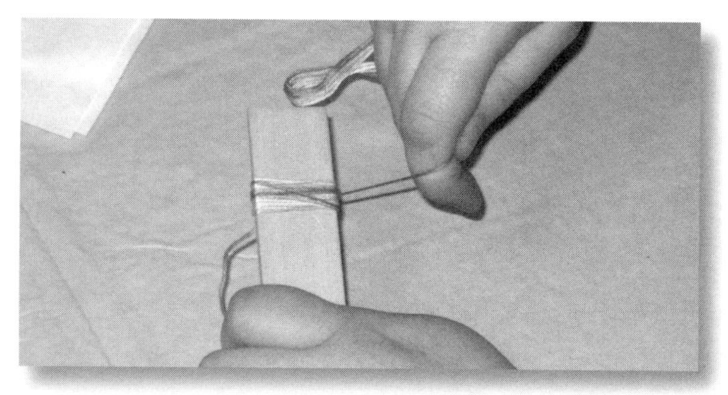

Making the tassel: Wrapping embroidery floss around ruler end

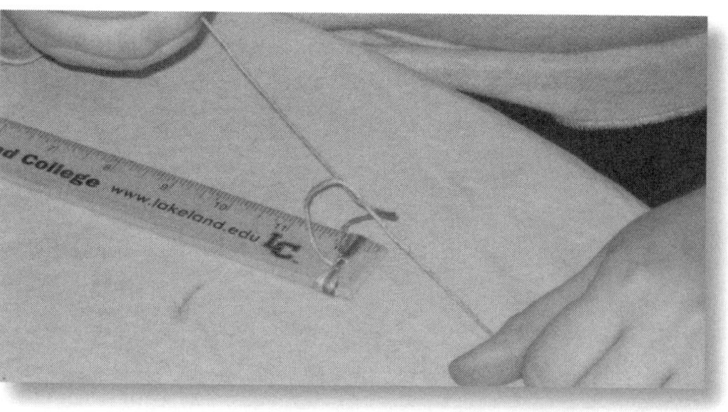

Making the tassel: Tying off wrapped coils of floss

Making the tassel: Cutting the coils from the ruler end

Making the tassel: Knotting the floss at the base of the tassel

If the crayon shavings aren't melting the way you'd like, try running the iron directly over the parchment paper. Be careful, though, of any wax running out from under the paper.

Repeat steps 2 and 3 as needed until you get the desired effect.

Step 4: Gluing

After letting your bookmark cool briefly, remove the masking tape and fold along the crease. Apply glue with the glue stick to the inside of the bookmark. Fold over and glue together. This should give you a cleaner back and a stronger bookmark.

Step 5: Embellishing

Add character to your bookmark with embellishments. Use the markers to draw or write your own quotes, or use white glue to attach vellum quotes and other decorations (e.g., sequins, small beads, etc.). Keep any three-dimensional embellishment small and lightweight so as not to damage the book or make the bookmark too heavy to use.

Step 6: Tasseling

To make a tassel, wrap twine or embroidery floss around a ruler or a square of cardboard (1 inch wide at least), leaving a 4½-inch-long tail at the lead-in.

Wrap ten to fifteen times, leaving another 4½-inch-long tail on the end. Clip off the excess. Loop the tails under the wrapped strands and bring them back around to tie a knot, gathering the wrapped strands together. Knot the tails at their loose ends and clip short. Turn over the ruler or cardboard and clip the wrapped strands in the middle.

Punch a hole at the top center of your bookmark. Thread the tassel tail through the hole. Using a slipknot, attach the tassel to the bookmark.

Note: You may need to demonstrate how to do this.

Attaching the tassel to the bookmark using a slipknot

Spin-offs

Note cards, reading journal covers.

Adaptations

Because the project itself is so easy, you can adapt it to different groups by adding extra supervision or by using fatter crayons. Patrons with developmental disabilities will need more help and may need someone to iron their projects for them. For seniors or people with disabilities, fatter crayons will be easier to hold. You may also want to have tassels premade for these groups.

Notes

Pressed Flower Note Cards

Project 3

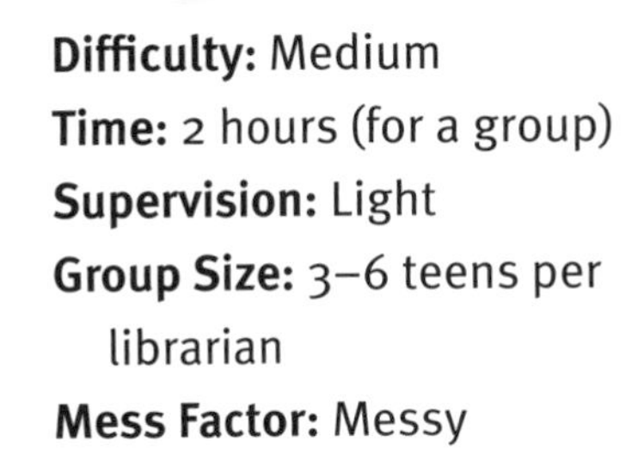

Difficulty: Medium
Time: 2 hours (for a group)
Supervision: Light
Group Size: 3–6 teens per librarian
Mess Factor: Messy

Finished pressed flower note cards

DRYING FLOWERS IS a traditional crafting staple. Using this process and creating note cards with flourishes of scrapbooking techniques and stamping update this staple into a chic new project.

Although it may take a few tries to get the knack of creating these designer-look note cards, the result is really worth the trouble. Teens will come away with not only a nice stack of beautiful stationery but also a new appreciation for the flowers and foliage in their own area.

These note cards, or any of the project variations, can work well with various types of library programs. The project can be used to highlight recycling issues or environmentalism, or even be part of your spring programming. The techniques may also be of interest to any scrapbooking groups or gardening groups that meet regularly at your library.

This project can be used in conjunction with service projects—cards for shut-ins, thank-you cards to the Friends of the Library for helping to fund a teen program, or thank-you cards for performers or authors who come to the library. If the products are stellar, the teen group or Friends of the Library could sell them in conjunction with a fund-raiser or book sale.

A printable one-page instruction sheet for this program is available on the book's website: www.ala.org/editions/extras/Coleman09713.

Supplies and Tools

burnishing tools (1 for each participant)
craft knives
glue sticks
ink pads
markers
newspaper
packing tape (clear)
pencils

phone books
rubber stamps (letter stamps come in handy)
scissors
scrapbooking punches
scrapbooking scissors
Styrofoam trays
tape dispensers (at least 1 for every 2 people in the group)
tissues or makeup sponges

Materials

blank note cards
card stock
pressed flowers (see how-to below)
scrapbooking vellum pages
vellum pages with quotations or words (available in some craft stores)

Room Requirements

2 tables (both covered with newspaper or drop cloth)
2 large wastebaskets (one at either end of the main table)
broom and dustpan (optional, but good to have on hand)

Prep Work

Getting the Flowers Ready

Here is the crux of this project—drying the flowers will take *at least two weeks*. Getting the teens involved in this part of the project can be worthwhile if it's practical.

Examples of flowers and leaves after pressing

Pick the flowers or leaves when the weather is dry (don't pick them in the rain or in the morning when they're covered in dew). Pay attention to color, structure, size, and texture. Thicker leaves with visible veins will work well (maple, lilac, ferns, ivy, etc.). Flowers with coarse seed heads are not very easy to work with. Houseplants are also good candidates (African violets, poinsettias, etc.). Even if you're unsure how well a plant will dry, it's worth trying it out. Also remember to look at flowers and plants all through the year because they can look dramatically different depending on the season. Sometimes colors can change considerably in the drying process, so choosing a variety of plants will give you more options later.

To dry the flowers and leaves, first arrange them on sheets of newspaper. Don't overlap; flowers and leaves should not be touching each other, but complete surfaces should be in contact with the newspaper. Fold the newspaper sheets enough to fit into the phone book. The more pressure on the flowers the better your results will be, so you may want to use several books with a few flowers in each one and stack to store. Leave the flowers to dry in the phone books at least two weeks. After drying, the flowers can be stored indefinitely in a cool, dry place.

You can use this project as a three-week program by having the teens pick and dry the flowers and leaves in the first week. In the second week, incorporate a guest speaker (topics can range from ecology to poetry), or have the teens draw flowers and leaves from reference books or find quotations and sayings that they would like to use on their note cards. Then complete the note cards in the third week.

Getting the Room Ready

This project can get pretty cluttered, so you'll want enough space to keep supplies and materials organized. The best way to store the flowers is to leave them in the phone books, so you'll need space for browsing. Teens can use the Styrofoam trays to organize their selected flowers. Phone books with the flowers, blank note cards, card stocks, and the scrapbooking pages should be kept on a side table that's easy to access but that keeps them out of the way. The other supplies and materials can be left on the group table for everyone to use as needed.

Directions

Step 1: Rummaging and Planning

Rummage through the flowers and other embellishing materials. Once you have your cards, flowers, and vellums (if needed), you're ready to plan. You'll want to play around with the layout to see what you like before you stick anything down.

Drawing details to turn a cloverleaf into a butterfly

The cards will look better if they aren't completely covered by tape. Also, keep this tip in mind: the fewer tape seams, the better. Tape seams can be the beginning of a lot of problems. If the tape doesn't meet up at the seam all the way, the flower will crack apart there. If the seam develops a wrinkle, it can be impossible to get that wrinkle out. So plan your work accordingly.

Here are a few design tips:

Card stock in a contrasting color and cut into a nice shape can work well as a backdrop and add dimension to your design.

Grouping flowers or leaves by size or color can create good patterns.

If you're planning to cover the entire face of the card and flower with vellum, check to make sure enough of the detail will show through.

Large flowers or leaves look better placed singly on a card.

Smaller flowers or leaves can be used singly or grouped at an edge or in a corner.

If you want to use any of the vellum quotes or plan to stamp words onto your card, be sure to plan for that in your layout.

Keep in mind that your flowers and leaves don't always have to be "flowers" or "leaves." With the right shape and a little imagination, you can use them to suggest butterflies or fairies.

Step 2: Sticking

Once you have a layout you like, you're ready to stick things down. There are three basic techniques for this step and each has variations.

STICKING ONTO CARD STOCK

If you're planning to make a lot of cards, this is the easiest technique to assembly-line. Cut your card stock to size and shape using the scrapbook edging scissors or by carefully ripping or even using straight-edge scissors, depending on the effect you want. Then use the glue stick to put a small amount of glue only on the area where the flower is to be. This glue is only to hold the flower in place while you tape it down, so you don't need a lot. Next, take a strip of packing tape. Working horizontally, gently place the tape over the flower. The tape should cover the flower but be securely on the card stock as well. The tape should overlap the flower at least ¼ inch. Handle the tape gingerly and as precisely as possible. The dried flowers can be very delicate. Repeat this process of taping until the flower is completely taped to the card stock. Once it's covered, use the craft knife to trim off any rough edges of tape before burnishing the tape down.

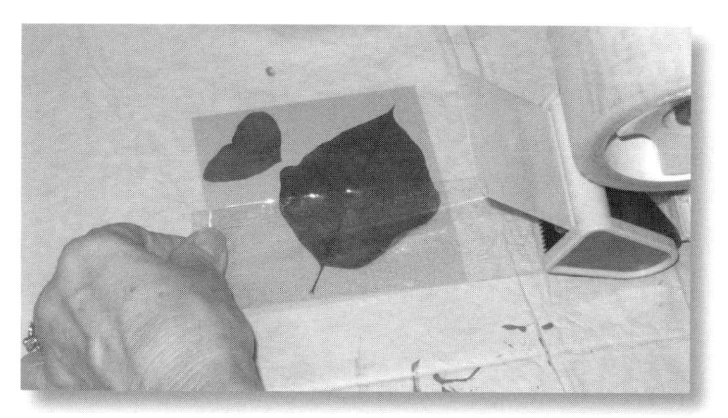

Applying tape to laminate

This technique works well for large arrangements of many flowers or plants that spread out across the card. For these larger arrangements, you may want to use a larger piece of card stock than you need and cover it completely. Once the tape is burnished down, you can trim around your arrangement.

Once you're finished trimming the card stock, use the glue stick to glue it onto the note card.

Gluing finished cardstock piece to the blank note card

STICKING DIRECTLY ONTO THE NOTE CARD

This process is almost the same as sticking the flower to the card stock, but it's a little riskier—if you make a mistake, you sacrifice an entire card. Once you have the flower in place on the front of the note card, use the glue stick to put a small amount of glue only on the area where the flower is to be. This glue is only to hold the flower in place while you tape it down, so you don't need a lot. Working horizontally, gently place a strip of packing tape over the flower. The tape should cover the flower but be securely on the note card as well. The tape should overlap the flower by at least ¼ inch. Handle the tape gingerly and as precisely as possible. The dried flowers can be very delicate. Repeat this process of taping until the flower is completely taped down on the note card. Once it's covered, use the craft knife to trim off any rough edges of tape before burnishing the tape down. This technique is best used only on a small area like corners or edges.

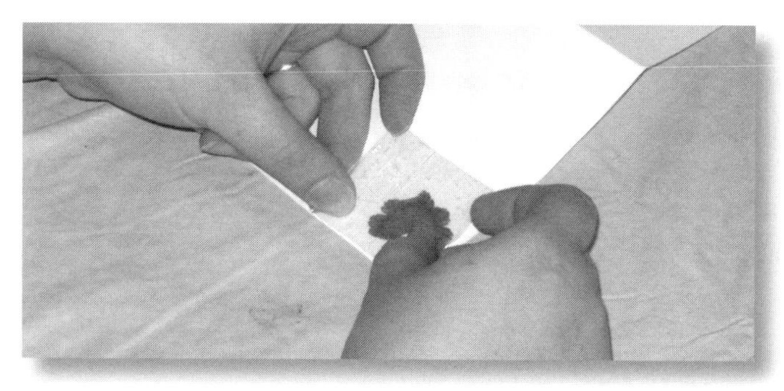

Using tape to laminate a small section of the card

Burnishing tape firmly

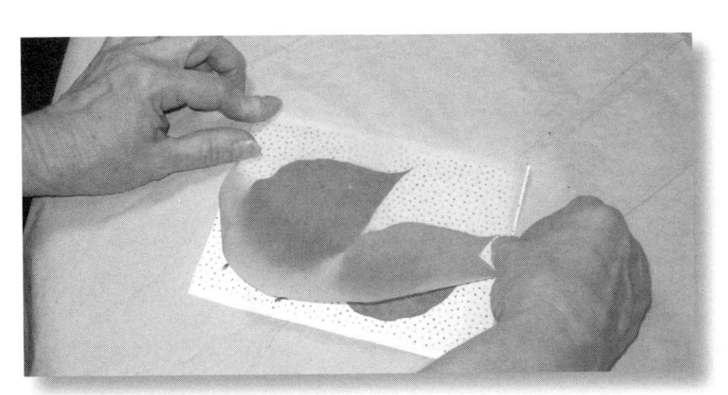

Applying vellum overlay

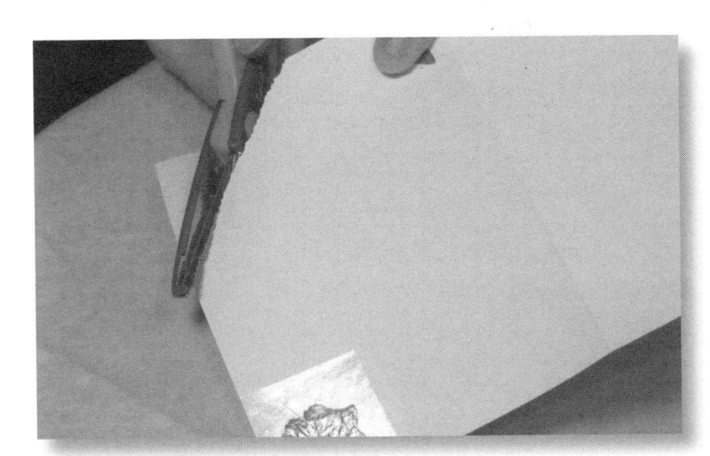

Cutting decorative edges

Applying ink to cut edge

COVERING WITH VELLUM

This technique works best if you cover the entire face of the card (and flower, of course) with vellum. The vellum is translucent and adds a soft, muted look to the flowers. It comes in many colors and patterns, so you have plenty of options for this look. Keep in mind, though, that vellum-covered cards leave little room for other types of embellishment.

Once you've decided on placement, cut the vellum to size. It should be either exactly the same size as the face of the card or slightly smaller. Use the glue stick to put a small amount of glue only on the area where the flower is to be. Put the flowers in place and press them down gently to secure them. Next, cover one side of the vellum with glue from the glue stick. Then, glue side down, place the vellum over the flowers and onto the card face. Smooth down gently.

Step 3: Embellishing

There are various techniques for embellishing these cards. You can add words by gluing on quotes or using stamped words or letters. Use the scrapbooking scissors or careful tearing to add interesting edges. You can also use the stamp pad ink with the tissues or sponges to add color and dimension. To highlight the edges with ink, brush an inked tissue or sponge across the edge lightly. Use decorative stamps or scrapbook punches to add shapes and designs.

Spin-offs

Bookmarks, scrapbooks, book covers, displays.

Notes

Blank Books

Difficulty: Medium–hard
Time: 30–90 minutes
Supervision: Medium
Group Size: 6–8 teens
Mess Factor: Messy

Finished blank books

BLANK BOOKS MAKE a perfect project for teens to show off their individuality and creativity. Blank books can be used for photo albums, scrapbooks, journals, and address books. Here we're using a few basic bookbinding techniques, but keep in mind that this is an old and storied art form. There are some very good books on bookbinding and its history, and you should encourage teens to look for these books in the library. Or you could bring some of these books to the craft program for inspiration and to give teens a sense of how far they could take the project.

The project is a natural fit for the library and can be worked into several types of programs. Book groups can use this craft to make book journals. You can have teens make books as a part of back-to-school programming or to use as a photo album at the end of the school year. Or you can make the books as a part of a poetry program. You can use the craft as a parent-child activity to make a scrapbook or as part of a reading program. Or have teens in a manga or anime group make them with the binding on the right side for a manga doodle pad or sketchbook.

Here, we'll present instructions for four types of blank books: ring bound, sewn, glued in, and accordion folded. These are all basic techniques that should give your teens enough options to create several different books.

A printable one-page instruction sheet for this program is available on the book's website: www.ala.org/editions/extras/Coleman09713.

Supplies and Tools

binder clips
box cutter
brads
cutting board (wood is better)
finishing nail (small) and a hammer
hole punches (have as many as possible on hand)

large needle
markers
paintbrushes
paper cutter (optional)
pen
pencils
rulers
scissors (straight-edge and scrapbooking)
small cups
Styrofoam trays
tape
tissues or makeup sponges
white glue

Materials

binding rings
card and paper stock
cardboard (thick enough to act as book covers; various textures are nice)
decorative papers (wallpaper, wrapping paper, origami paper, etc.)
embroidery floss
paint (watercolor or acrylic)
paper scrap
ribbon
rubber stamps and ink pads
stencils and stencil paint
twine

Room Requirements

2 tables
large wastebasket
several small wastebaskets

Prep Work

Getting the Project Ready

Precut the cardboard, card stock, and paper stock. Cut pieces to 11 by 14 inches, 8 by 10 inches, 5 by 7 inches, 4 by 4 inches, and 6 by 6 inches so participants can have a choice of sizes. Remember that the interior pages should be slightly smaller than the book covers, so cut the paper stock about ¼ inch smaller than the cardboard on all sides. Organize the materials into separate piles on the side table.

Getting the Room Ready

Lay out tools and supplies on a side table. Cover the worktable with a drop cloth or newspaper. Place small wastebaskets at each end and side of the worktable, and keep the large wastebasket centrally located.

Getting Supplies Ready

At the worktable, set up a Styrofoam tray at each work space (allow plenty of room for each participant to work on cutting and gluing). Everyone should also have a ruler, pen, pencil, small cup, paintbrushes, scissors, and instructions. Place markers, paint, glue, extra paintbrushes, and hole punches in the center of the table.

Directions

Step 1: Planning and Selecting Materials

Have the participants read the instructions and decide on a plan for their book. They may want to think about how they will use their book and then decide on the size, type of binding, and materials they will need.

Once they have a design in mind, they can go to the materials table to pick out their book covers, paper or card stock, and decorating supplies.

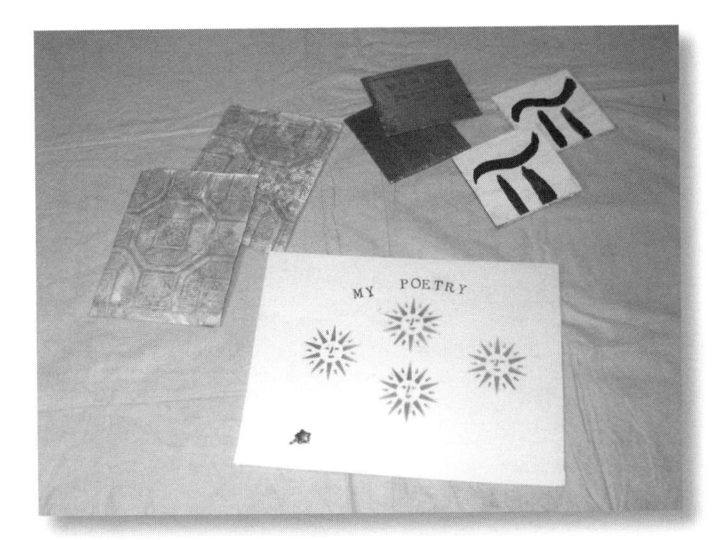

Finished book covers, showing examples of stamped, painted, decoupaged, and stained-wallpaper covers

Step 2: Designing the Covers

This is the chance to be creative and make the book individual to yourself and the book's planned use. You can really do anything you want with the cover. Make it as simple or as complex as you'd like. We'll go over a few basics, but remember that you can mix and match these ideas or even do something else entirely.

DRAWING OR PAINTING

You can draw or trace a picture onto the cover and paint with watercolor or acrylic paint. Or you can use stencils to create a design. Layer your designs if you'd like, making sure to let the paint dry between layers. Also, make sure your covers are completely dry before you go on to binding.

Finished interior pages, loose and accordion

DECOUPAGING

You can overlay the book cover with words or pictures cut from magazines, books, newspapers, or comics. You can even use less traditional paper scrap, such as wallpaper scraps, wrapping paper, or origami paper. Again, layering can create a nice effect. Let the decoupage medium dry completely before binding.

STAMPING, USING MARKERS, AND MORE

You can create designs with rubber stamps and stamping ink or markers or both. You can also add interest by using cardboard with different textures. Try combining some of these techniques to create even more detailed designs. Don't forget to decorate the inside of the cover as well!

You can also embellish the pages. Try using scrapbooking scissors to cut different types of edges, or rip the edges. Sponge ink onto the pages or use stencils and rubber stamps to add designs.

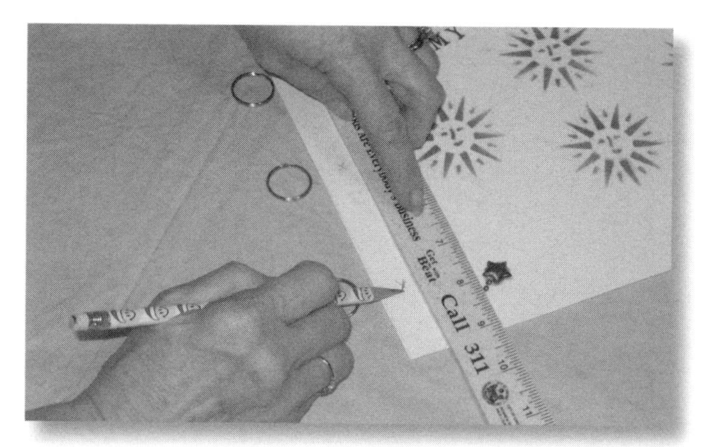

Ring binding: Measuring and marking location of the holes on the cover

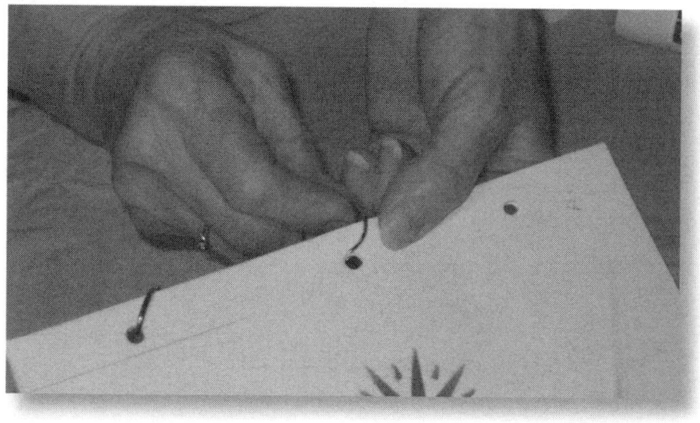

Ring binding: Adding rings

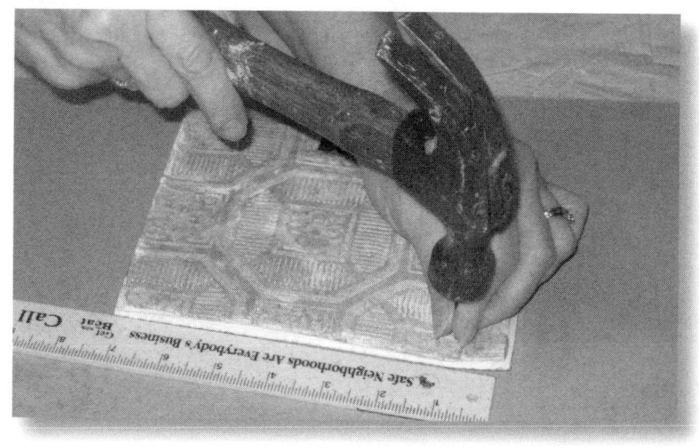

Sewn binding: Making holes with hammer and nail

Step 3: Binding

BINDING 1: RING BOUND

Ring binding is the most basic binding short of stapling your book together at the corners. It can be used to good effect, though, depending on how you plan to use the book and where you place the rings.

Decide which edge is going to be the back or bound edge of your covers and your paper stock. Using a ruler, mark the placement of the holes. For consistency and ease of hole punching, do the covers first. Measure in from the edge at least ½ inch but no more than 1 inch (unless you're making a really huge book) and mark this spot. Do this at the top, middle, and bottom of the cover. Draw a line through all three marks. Next, measure along this line to place the marks where the holes should be punched.

Punch the holes in the first cover, and then use it as a guide to mark the other cover and the paper stock.

Remember that the binding is a part of your design, so you should try to add interest with it. For example, rather than doing a standard three-ring bind at even intervals, measure and mark holes for six rings. Or place holes so you'll have two rings close together at the top, one in the middle, and two more close together at the bottom. Also, keep in mind that your book does not have to open left to right. Your binding can be at the top or bottom or even on the right edge.

Once all the pages and the covers are punched, insert the rings and close them. The size of the rings you use will depend on the thickness of your book. Binding rings are the obvious choice, but you don't have to use them. You can also tie through the holes with ribbon or twine, or you can even use shower curtain rings.

BINDING 2: SEWN

Once you have your covers and pages designed and you know which edge you are going to bind, stack them in the order you want them to be bound and clip them together tightly with binder clips at the top and bottom. The pages and covers need to be held securely together.

Measure and mark where to put the holes.

With the cutting board underneath the book, use the hammer and finishing nail to make the holes. The holes need to be big enough for the string you plan to use to pass through. This technique works best if you plan to have just a few spots of lacing at the back.

When all the holes have been made, thread a large-eye needle with string and lace through the holes, making sure your lacing is secure. Be sure to leave a tail at the beginning so you can tie it off. Your goal is to go into the first hole, then go through all the others in whatever pattern you prefer, and make it back to the first hole, leaving another tail to tie.

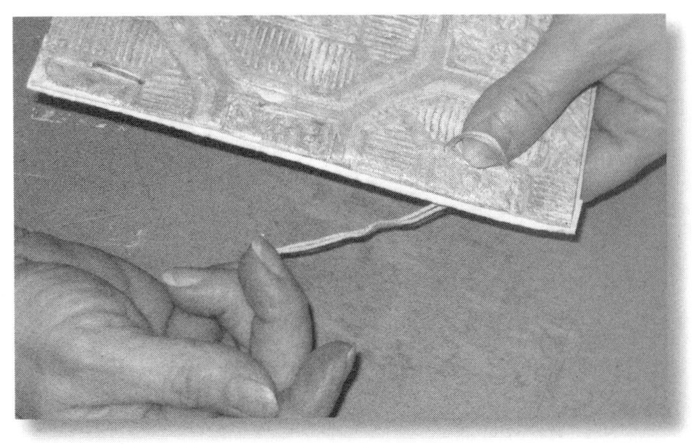
Sewn binding: Using needle and thread to sew through holes

BINDING 3: GLUED IN

For a glued-in binding, you bind your pages first and then glue them into the covers with an endpaper. This should be the most familiar example. If you are using this binding method, you can skip the step of decorating the interior of the covers. The endpapers will be your interiors.

Start with your interior pages. Stack them and clip them together with binder clips at the top and bottom. Measure ¼ inch in from the edge to be bound and draw a line down the top page. Next, make marks on the line at 1-inch intervals. Then, with the cutting board under your pages, use the hammer and nail to make holes at your marks.

When all the holes have been made, sew the pages together with embroidery floss.

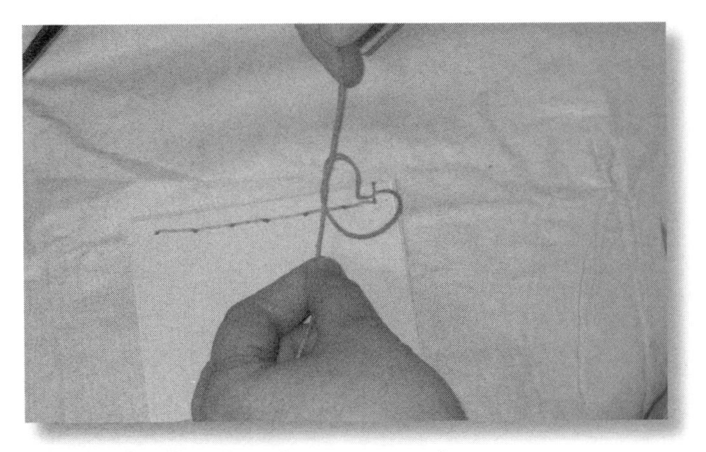
Glued-in binding: Securing sewn-together interior pages with a knot

When the pages are sewn together, prepare your endpapers. To get the dimensions, measure across the front page and add that to the measurement across the front cover. The height will be the same as the height of your interior pages. You'll need two endpapers.

When you have your endpapers cut, fold them in half. Glue one half to the top interior page and the other half to the inside cover. Do this for both covers. Now you should have what looks like a book with no spine.

To add a spine to the book, you can use either a scrap of fabric, a piece of wide ribbon, or even paper scrap. Cut the spine piece to overlap the covers by at least 1 inch. Once you have it cut, glue it in place with decoupage medium or white glue.

If you want to cheat the spine, you can use duct tape.

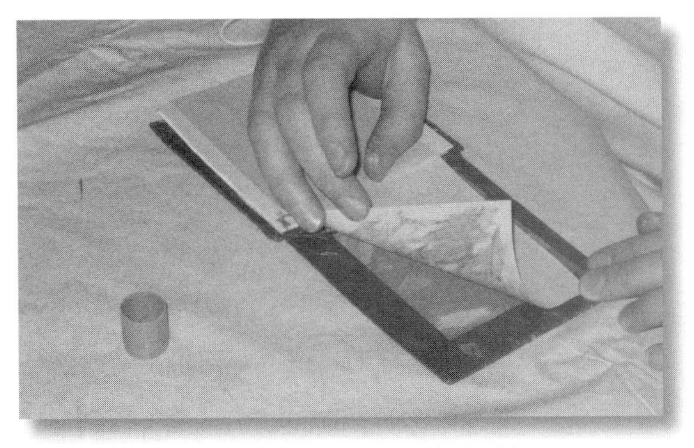
Glued-in binding: Gluing endpaper to the inside cover

BINDING 4: ACCORDION

Accordion binding works best with small, square books (4 by 4 inches to 6 by 6 inches). The hardest part of this binding technique is making sure you have a piece of paper long enough to make several pages. Large pads of watercolor or other art paper will work well. If you want a lot of pages, you can cut the paper into strips of the appropriate width and glue them together end to end.

The pages of this book are part of the binding, so we will go over the instructions here.

The pages should be ½ inch smaller than the covers. For this example we will be making a 4-by-4-inch book, with pages that will be 3½ by 3½ inches. The pages are also one long strip.

Accordion binding: Interior page strip, with folds

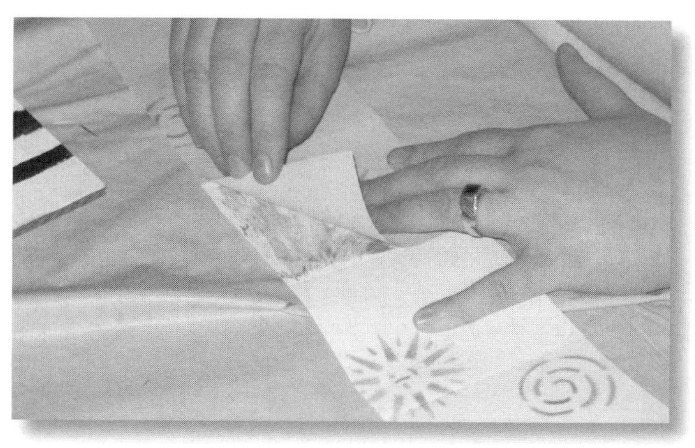

Accordion binding: Gluing page strips together to make more pages

Accordion binding: Gluing end page to inside cover

Accordion binding: Finished book, with pages extended

To start, take a long strip of paper that is 3½ inches wide. Mark and fold this strip at 3½-inch intervals. Snip off any excess paper.

If you want to add more pages, cut another strip of 3½-inch-wide paper and fold it in the same way, again snipping off any excess. When you have your two little accordions, match the last fold on one with the first fold on the other. Glue these two "pages" together. This will give you one long strip of paper with 3½-inch folds all the way across.

Glue the first page onto the inside of the front cover and the last page onto the inside of the back cover.

If you don't like the way the pages look on the inside covers, you can decorate them however you'd like.

Now use the same hammer-and-nail technique from the sewn and glued bindings to add holes to the back edge of the *covers only*. Thread the holes with string or ribbon, and tie.

If you want a little closure for the book, add another set of holes at the front of the book covers and attach a ribbon on each cover to tie the book closed.

Notes

Layered Fabric Collages

Difficulty: Medium
Time: 30–60 minutes
Supervision: Light–medium
Group Size: 4–8 teens
Mess Factor: Messy

Finished fabric collage

THESE COLLAGES ARE a fun way to have your teens illustrate their favorite books. The project can be structured to fit various types of programs that you have planned.

You could use this project with your teen book group and have each participant create her or his own vision of the story. Or have each teen create a collage to illustrate different scenes or themes of the book. Or have participants collage their own interpretation of the same scene.

You could also use this project during your summer reading campaigns or with any teen reading programs by having your group create collages to illustrate one of the books they've read. Or they can design a collage postcard from their favorite fantasyland. You can also have the group collaborate on designing a large collage featuring several books or concentrating on just one group favorite.

This project can work well with reading buddy programs by having teens help younger children illustrate a book or books that they read together. You may want to suggest the idea to your teen group well beforehand to make sure they like the idea and understand the project before running the full program. If you use this project in this way, have the teens gather at least a half hour before the younger kids arrive so they can get supplies ready and review instructions. This would be especially fun for a group of teens who have done the collage project before.

You can also use this project with a more free-form approach, letting the teens pick their own book to illustrate and giving looser parameters for the project, such as interpreting the emotional themes or illustrating the story from a specific character's point of view. You can even use the project with a teen writing group by having participants build their story with the collage.

Whatever the programming behind the project, your teens will end up with some very creative results that can be displayed in the library or taken home.

A printable one-page instruction sheet for this program is available on the book's website: www.ala.org/editions/extras/Coleman09713.

Supplies and Tools

brushes
carbon paper
markers
pencils
poster board
rulers
scissors
white glue

Materials

embellishments
fabric scraps
found objects
paper scraps
resource pictures or original drawings

Room Requirements

2 tables (main activity table covered with newspaper or drop cloth)
large wastebasket
several small wastebaskets to share

Prep Work

Getting the Project Ready

The most basic way to approach this project is to have pictures ready for your group to choose from. These pictures can be pulled from several sources, such as coloring books, iconic book covers, and illustrations. It is important to find pictures with clear-cut line work that will look good in blocks of color. You may want to avoid images with a lot of small details like faces or intricate line work. If you're using this approach, have your teens select their pictures first.

Another approach that may yield more creative results but will also take more time and prep work is to have your teens draw an original plan for their collage. In either case, the picture or drawing should have clear-cut lines and not a lot of fine detail. It may be helpful to show your teens some pictures of the finished examples (available in color online at www.arystocrafts.com). For some participants these collages may work better if they are a more symbolic representation of the themes of the story rather than a literal interpretation, and you may need to offer a little direction to that effect.

Once you have the pictures in hand (either drawn or ready-made), each participant will need at least five copies of her or his picture in order to build up the layers of the collage.

Getting the Room Ready

This project can get messy, especially with a larger group. The best setup we've found is to put fabric and paper scraps, found objects, and embellishments on a side counter or table. That way, teens can take only what they need back to the main table.

The main table should be equipped with white glue, brushes, scissors, and carbon paper for each participant. Each participant should be a part of the group, but still have enough room to work comfortably.

Getting Supplies Ready

Each participant will need his or her own piece of 11-by-14-inch poster board. Have materials and supplies on hand and easily accessible. Fabric scraps should be loosely piled or in a container large enough to rummage through. Found objects and other embellishments are easier to see if they are sorted in some manner (e.g., by color or size) or also in a large container to be rummaged through freely.

Directions

Step 1: Choosing Your Picture

Have participants choose a picture from the group you've supplied, or have them draw their own. Remember to share the guidelines on what makes a good image for this project to avoid frustrations later, and make sure participants follow them.

Step 2: Collecting Materials

After participants choose or finish designing their picture and listen to your basic instructions and explanation of the project, give them time to do a preliminary rummage at the materials table. They should pick out their main fabrics, and if they see some found pieces they absolutely have to use, they can lay claim to them.

If you're tight for space, you may have participants rummage two or three at a time. In the meantime, those at the main table can be planning how they want their finished piece to look.

Step 3: Building the Background

Using the carbon paper, trace the basic background lines of your picture onto the poster board. You don't need to trace the entire picture just yet.

Once you have the background lines (if any) in place, choose your first layer of fabrics. Clip the fabric scraps to fit your background. As you're working with the background, play around with textures or tones. A sky can be made of various tones of blue, white, and gray, or grass can be suggested in a fabric's texture or pattern. Be sure to plan carefully before gluing. Try moving things around or placing them at different angles.

Once you have your fabric where you like it, brush on a light coat of glue and stick the fabric down.

Background: Gluing down fabric pieces

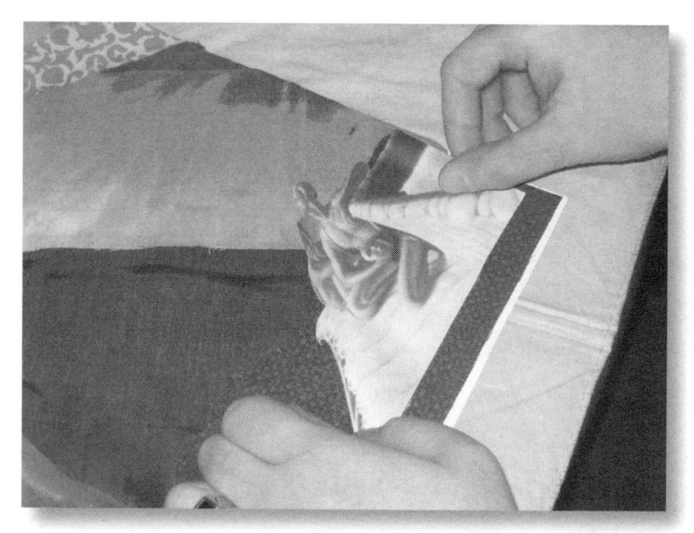

Layering: Building the second layer

Applying embellishments

Step 4: Building Up

Once you have your background glued down, any details of your picture are now covered in fabric. *Don't panic.* This is why you have more than one copy. Looking at your picture, decide what the next layer of the picture is. This layer should be the larger objects in your picture that are going to be fabric (e.g., houses, words, characters, etc.).

There are two ways to transfer these objects onto your background. You could use the carbon paper and trace the image directly onto the background. Once you have the image traced, cut out your fabric scraps and glue them into place. Or you could trace the image on the fabric scrap(s) you are creating the objects from, cut them out, then glue them onto the background. Allow the piece to dry for a few minutes between layers.

Repeat this layering technique until you have finished all the pieces of your collage that you want to create in fabric. Building up the layers adds texture and dimension to the finished piece. All the main lines of your objects should be fabric.

Step 5: Embellishing

The smaller details of the collage can now be created with embellishments. Create signs with pictures or words cut from magazines in your paper scrap; fashion clock faces with watches. Beads in any color can be used to highlight and add dimension. You can also use markers to write messages.

Adaptations

This project can be adapted for different types of groups by changing the materials you make available. Younger kids or patrons with developmental disabilities can work well with this project if you provide them with a larger poster board and give them more hands-on help with cutting and gluing.

If you want to frame this project as a truly group endeavor, have your teens work on one large piece to use as a display for the teen area or as an art piece for the library in general.

Notes

Coasters and Trivets

Difficulty: Medium
Time: 2–4 hours
Supervision: Light–medium
Group Size: 6–8 teens per librarian
Mess Factor: Messy

Finished coaster tiles

THESE COASTERS AND trivets offer new ideas for an old project. Your teen group can create some funky usable art pieces for themselves or for gifts. Each participant should be able to create at least one trivet and two coasters in the session.

You can tie this project into a book group or use it as a summer reading program activity. Have teens select paper scrap that will enhance or illustrate the book, or have them use pictures from graphic novels or comics or maps. Words can also make creative designs. By using words in designs you can enhance your poetry group, or the teens can use words or expressions cut from magazines or books to create their own poetry on the coasters or trivets.

This is also a great holiday gift project. Have your teens make coasters or trivets for people on their own gift lists or to give to library staff, to elderly or shut-in patrons, or as a thank-you to speakers or guests. If your teen group is up for it, you can even use this project as a reading buddy activity, with the teens helping younger kids to create pieces from color copies of their favorite books.

A printable one-page instruction sheet for this program is available on the book's website: www.ala.org/editions/extras/Coleman09713.

Supplies and Tools

- beading or jewelry glue
- carbon paper
- masking tape
- nail polish remover or tile cleaner
- paintbrushes of various sizes
- paper towels
- pencils
- permanent markers
- rulers
- sandpaper
- scissors
- small paper cups
- small sponges
- stencils
- Styrofoam trays

Materials

- for coasters: white or very light colored ceramic wall tiles (4 inches by 4 inches)
- for trivets: white or very light colored floor tiles (12 inches by 12 inches)
- colored craft sand
- decoupage medium
- embellishments (sequins, small jewels, etc.)
- felt
- floral marbles
- glass paints
- glitter
- paper scrap
- polyurethane

Room Requirements

- 2 tables, covered
- large wastebasket
- several small wastebaskets

Prep Work

Getting the Project Ready

Gather and organize your supplies and materials. You will not need all the materials listed so you can select from what you have on hand. Organize the tiles according to size. Cut the felt into squares slightly smaller than the tiles.

Make a sample beforehand so participants can see the finished project.

Getting the Room Ready

Arrange paper scrap and embellishments in bins or containers. Keep all these supply items on a separate side table for teens to rummage through as needed. This will ensure that all your participants have enough room to work. If you are doing this craft as a reading buddy project, you may need an extra table to make sure each pair has room.

Cover your worktables with drop cloth or newspaper. Set each place with a Styrofoam tray that has project instructions, scissors, sandpaper, two small cups for water and decoupage, pencils, and a ruler. Place the assortment of paintbrushes, sponges, glass paints, masking tape, markers, and decoupage in the center of the table. Place small wastebaskets at each end and each side of the table, but keep the large wastebasket centrally located so participants can dispose of big messes easily.

Directions

Step 1: Planning the Design

Have the participants plan out their ideas either on paper or mentally so they can choose materials. There are several ways to approach the design of the trivets and coasters. You can use the glass paints to simply paint a freehand or abstract design, or you may want to stencil the tile. You can also use all paper scrap to produce your design. Of course, you can combine any or all of these techniques to create unique pieces.

Because the paints and decoupage dry quickly, suggest to participants that they plan the designs for each of their pieces at this point.

Step 2: Choosing Materials

When all the participants have their design(s) planned, they can go to the side table (two to four at a time works best) to select the materials they will use for their project. Remind the teens that they can return to the supply table whenever they need items, so they don't have to take everything for all three pieces right away.

Step 3: Prepping the Tiles

Lightly sand the tiles and clean them with the tile cleaner or nail polish remover. This step removes or dulls any finish on the tiles so the paint or decoupage will adhere better.

Step 4: Choosing Techniques

Your main design can be achieved by using several techniques. You can layer these techniques to get more varied results. For example, decoupage paper scrap, then dull it with a coat of watered-down paint for an aged look. Or stencil a design and highlight areas with glitter or sand. Layering can add more texture and depth to a design.

Creating a base layer: Painted tile

PAINTING

Lightly draw your design onto the tile. Remember to keep small details to a minimum. You can do this freehand or trace a picture using carbon paper.

Once you are satisfied with your drawing, begin filling in with the glass paint. The glass paint is translucent and appears too thin when first applied. When the paint is dry, you can add another coat if needed. Another approach is to use a small sponge to blend the color to get a muted effect and soften edges.

For an abstract design, just paint and blend colors until you get the effect you want.

Stencil applied over base layer

STENCILING

Choose your stencil and tape it into place with masking tape. Using a large stiff brush, a foam brush, or a sponge, dab paint onto the stencil making sure not to brush the paint. Allow the paint to dry a little and carefully remove the stencil.

PAPER SCRAP

Choose pictures or words and carefully cut them out. Apply decoupage medium to the tile and then place your pictures. Apply another coat of decoupage medium over the pictures. You can layer the pictures as much as you want.

COMBINATIONS

Your design may call for the use of some or all of these techniques. This sounds more complicated than it actually is and produces some very creative results. Paint your entire tile to give it a background color (you can use as many colors as you like for this). For example, you might want to use blue for sky or water, green for grass, yellow for the sun, and so on. While the paint dries, choose and cut out pictures from your paper scrap. Decoupage these into place, then add more splashes of paint to add color and interest and to build depth. Or use a stencil over the whole thing.

Remember, as one piece is drying, you can work on the other pieces you have planned.

Step 5: Embellishing

Once you have your base layers painted, decoupaged, and/or stenciled, you can add embellishments for your finishing touches. Embellishments should be simple and relatively flat. It wouldn't do to have a coaster that always overturned your cup of coffee.

Glitter and sand can be very effective for highlighting areas of your design or adding a subtle sparkle. Use them to fill in small areas or trace designs like smoke or clouds. Small sequins or jewels can also be added to give some sparkle and dimension. You can glue the glitter with decoupage, but make sure the rest of the tile is completely dry before sprinkling the glitter on so you can control where it goes. Glue the jewels or sequins down with beading or jewelry glue.

You can make fabulous embellishments by using permanent markers to outline important features of your design or to write words. Simply draw or trace with the marker, being very careful to keep your lines straight and steady.

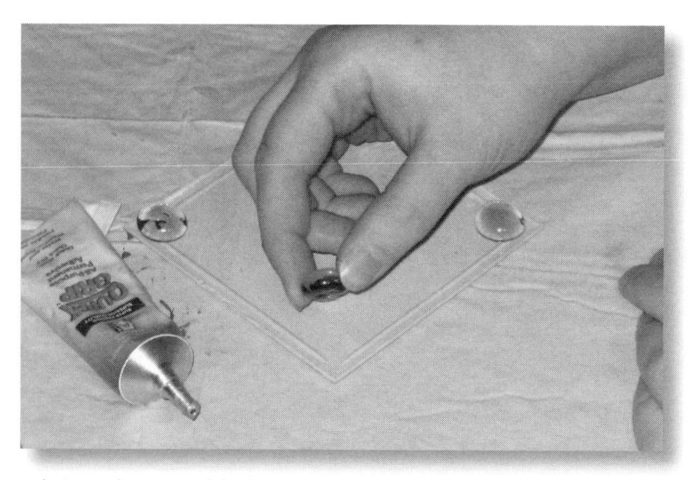

Gluing glass marble feet to the back of the finished tile

Step 6: Gluing the Bottom

When the tiles are completed and dry, glue the floral marbles to the bottom to form "feet." Using the beading or jewelry glue, put a floral marble on each corner of the underside of the tile.

If you'd rather not deal with the marbles, you can cut a square of felt slightly smaller than the tile and glue it to the bottom with the beading glue.

Step 7: Sealing

When your tile has dried, brush on a coat of polyurethane. Make sure to do this in a room with good ventilation. Let the first coat dry at least to a tacky finish and then give the tile at least one more coat to seal.

Note: If you are pressed for time, you can have the teens end with one coat of polyurethane. After it dries, you can add the second coat and have the coasters or trivets ready to be picked up at a subsequent meeting or at the reference desk.

Spin-offs

Trays, art pieces, pictures, garden stones.

Adaptations

This project can work well with younger kids or patrons who are developmentally disabled if you shrink the group size and limit the techniques and materials choices. It also works well for parent-child or senior groups.

Notes

Rubber Band Bracelets and Necklaces

Finished rubber band jewelry

Difficulty: Easy
Time: 30–60 minutes
Supervision: Light
Group Size: 6–8 teens
Mess Factor: None (unless there's a spontaneous rubber band fight)

THESE RUBBER BAND bracelets and necklaces are a simple, inexpensive, no-mess craft. The simplicity of the project allows for easy socializing among teens and little supervision once it is under way. This feature also makes the project easy to use in any existing crafting programs you may have planned. The basic supplies required make this project easy to work into programs dealing with recycling or environmentalism.

Depending on the rubber bands you use, these bracelets and necklaces will eventually deteriorate, although they should last for about six months, depending on how dry or brittle they get.

A printable one-page instruction sheet for this program is available on the book's website: www.ala.org/editions/extras/Coleman09713.

WEB

Supplies and Tools

dowels or pencils (1 for each participant)

Materials

beads (must have large holes)

small rubber bands (the best are the small "no-tangle" hair bands that are usually available in packs of 100)

Room Requirements

table
wastebasket

Prep Work

Getting the Project Ready

Put rubber bands and beads in containers large enough for participants to see what colors are available and take what they need. You may want to whip up a sample so teens can see how the project is supposed to look. You may want to have photocopies of the instructions available at the table as well.

Getting the Room Ready

Put the supplies out on a large table in your teen or YA area and let participants come and go as they please. Each participant will need a short dowel or pencil to use as an anchor.

There are two variations on this project that require different steps, so you'll want to choose between them at the beginning.

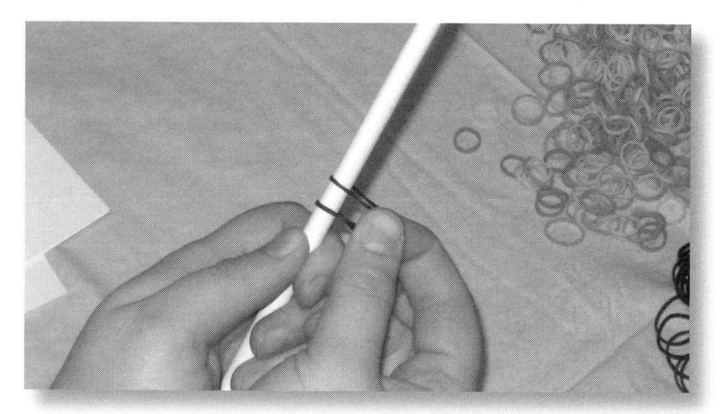

Folding the rubber band around the pencil to make the first link

Directions: Without Bead

Step 1: Beginning the Chain

Fold a rubber band around the dowel or pencil so you have two loops, one on either side of the dowel.

Slipping the rubber band through the loop ends of the first link to make the second link

Step 2: Extending the Chain

Thread a second rubber band through these two loops and pull it forward so you have another two loops. Essentially you are creating a chain with rubber bands. The dowel will act as an anchor on one end.

Continue adding rubber bands until you get the length of chain that you want (necklace, bracelet, anklet, etc.).

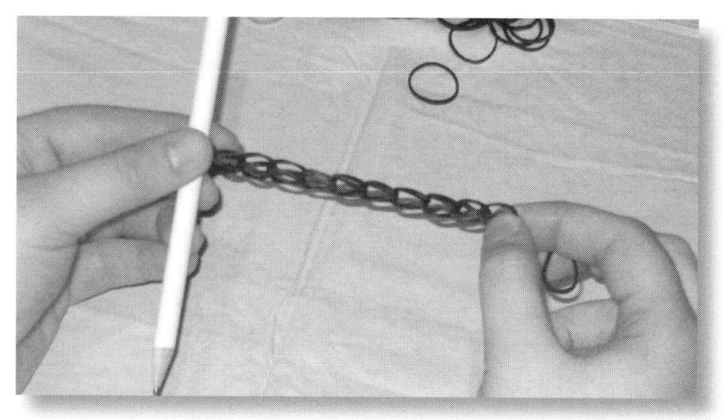

Continuing the chain

Step 3: Closing the Chain

When you have the desired length, you're ready to close off your chain. Slip the ends off the dowel or pencil carefully, making sure your chain doesn't unravel. You should have two loops at either end of your chain. Gather all four loops together and thread a new rubber band through all four. Instead of leaving the loops at the end of this new rubber band, pull one loop through the other to create a knot. Pull tightly. Done!

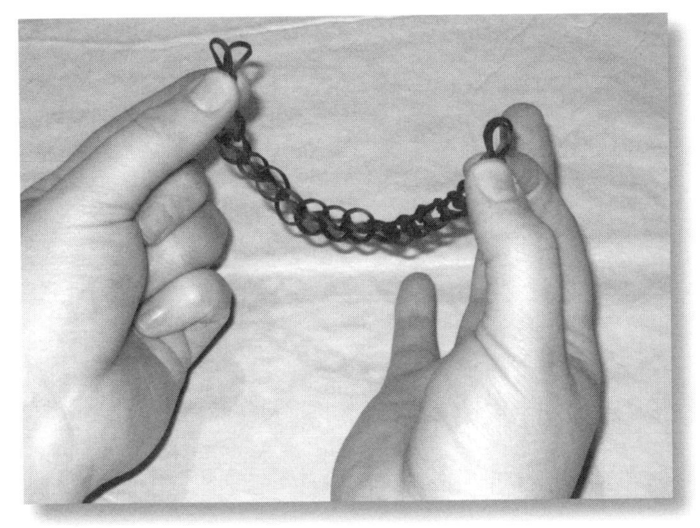

Finished chain ready to join at the ends

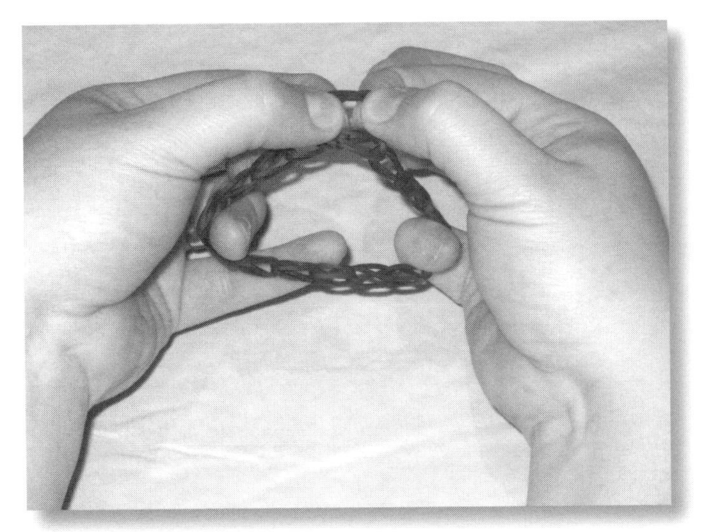

Holding the loops of both end links together, with loops lined up

Holding the loops of both end links together (left hand), with loops lined up

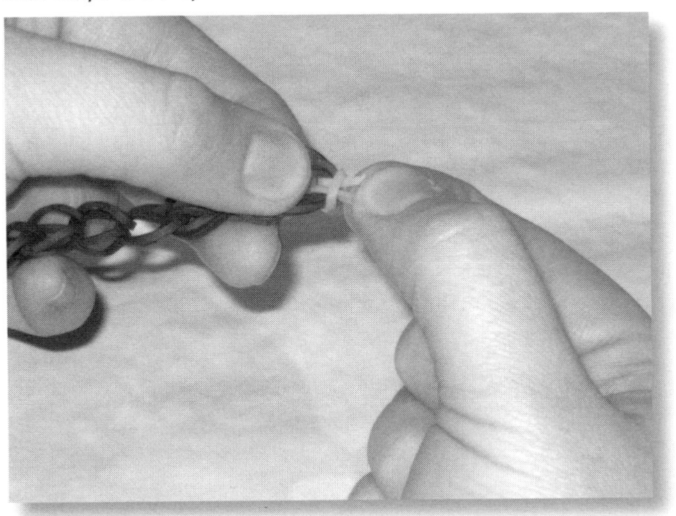

Closing the chain: Tying a rubber band in a slipknot through all the loops

Directions: Adding a Bead

There are three variations on this project that allow you to add a bead to your bracelet or necklace.

Option 1: Plain Beading

After your chain has five or six links, carefully thread the beads onto the chain, and then continue with the steps above until finished.

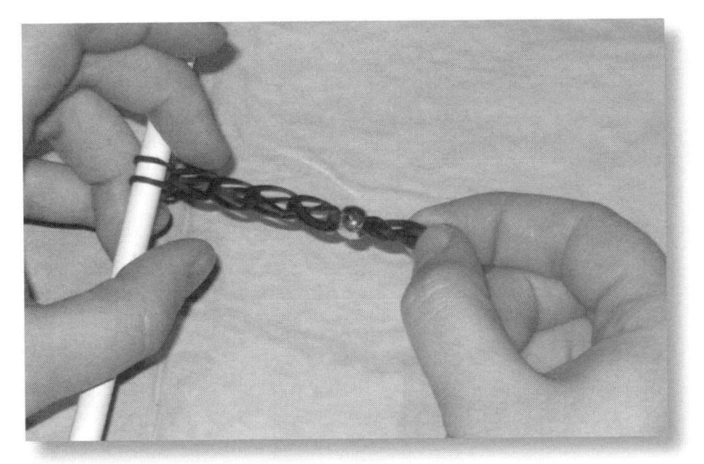

Beading technique 1: Sliding a bead onto a chain

Beading technique 2: Threading the first link rubber band through the bead, leaving a loop on either side of the bead

Beading technique 2: Anchoring the first link to the pencil on one side of the bead and continuing the chain from the loop on the other side of the bead

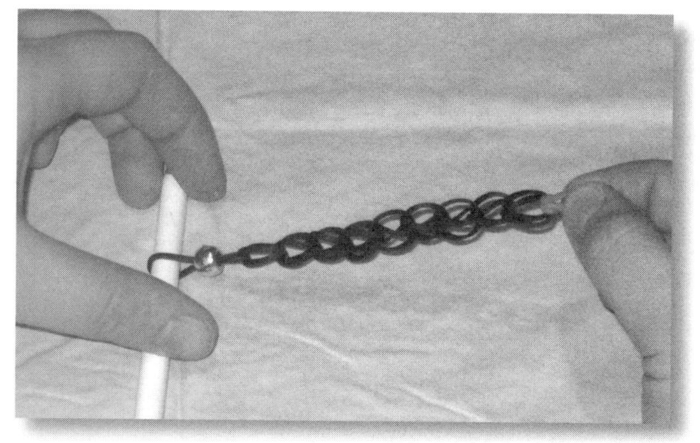

Beading technique 2: Temporarily tying off the first end at the halfway point

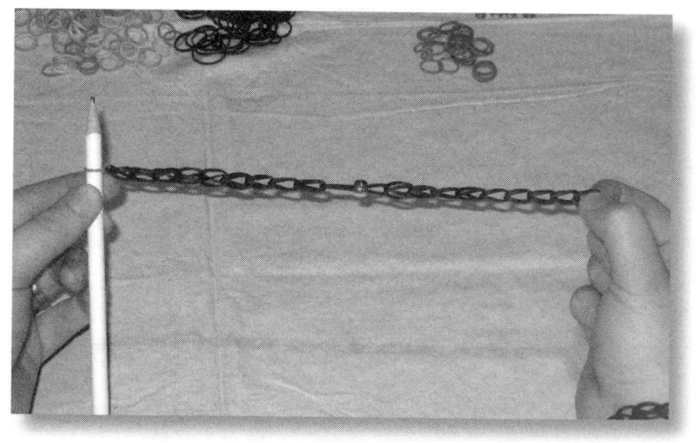

Beading technique 2: The entire chain, anchored to the pencil by the temporary tie-off band, with the beaded band in the center

Beading technique 2: Tying off the ends to close the bracelet

Option 2: Horizontal Beading

In this variation the bead has to be added at the beginning. If the bead is longer than the rubber bands you're using for the linking process, you may need to use a larger band for this part. Thread a rubber band through the bead. You should have a loop on either side. Thread a second rubber band through one side and pull both ends so you have two loops. Slide these loops onto your dowel to use as an anchor. Thread another band through the loop at the other end and continue building your chain as explained above.

Because you'll want the bead to end up in the front center of your bracelet or necklace, build the chain to reach half the distance needed, then tie it off temporarily. Slide the other side off the dowel or pencil and build the chain in the other direction until you have the same number of links on either side of the bead. When you're done with both sides, tie the whole piece off in the manner described above.

Beading technique 3: The bead is threaded with two bands, each looped in opposite directions.

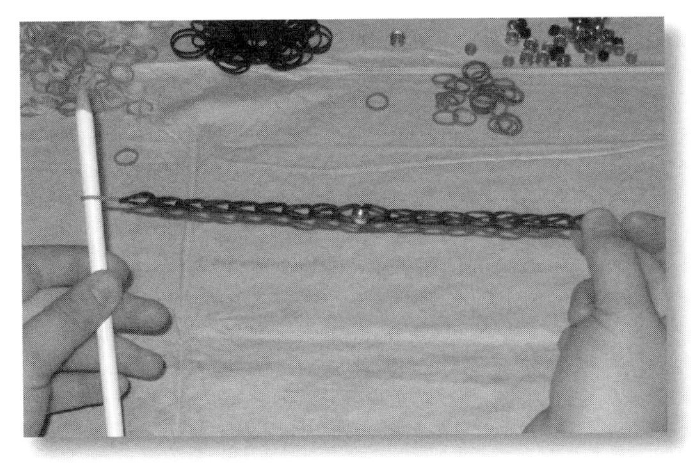

Beading technique 3: The first link anchors the piece to the pencil.

Beading technique 3: The chain is half completed and tied off on one end temporarily.

Beading technique 3: The entire chain, anchored to the pencil by the temporary tie-off band, with the bead in the center

Option 3: Vertical Beading

In this variation the bead has to be added at the beginning. Thread a rubber band through the bead, leaving a loop on either side. Pull the ends forward so you have two loops, one on the top and one on the bottom of the bead. Thread a second rubber band through these loops and slide the loops of this second rubber band onto your dowel or pencil to use as an anchor. Thread another band through the bead so you have two rubber bands through the hole. Again, pull the ends so you have two loops and thread another band through these. Build the chain in the same manner as before.

Because you'll want the bead to end up in the front center of your bracelet or necklace, build the chain to reach half the distance needed, then tie it off temporarily. Slide the other side off the dowel or pencil and build the chain in the other direction until you have the same number of links on either side of the bead. When you're done with both sides, tie the whole piece off in the manner described above.

Beading technique 3: Tying off the ends to close the bracelet

Add-ons (optional)

When you have your bracelet or necklace tied off, you can add additional beads and links for a dangling or charm-bracelet effect.

To do this, take the tail of the tie-off band and use the same technique to tie another band to it. Once you have it as long as you want, slide some beads on. Make a knot at the end big enough to stop the beads from coming off.

Spin-offs

Cell-phone charms, bookmarks, hair ties.

Adaptations

You can adapt this project easily for younger patrons or patrons with developmental disabilities simply by using larger rubber bands and beads. Make sure the bands are relatively short so they can make a chain. You may want to offer younger participants or those with disabilities more supervision to make sure the bracelets and necklaces aren't too tight.

Notes

Mosaic Tile Jewelry

Difficulty: Medium
Time: Two 90-minute sessions
Supervision: Medium
Group Size: 3–6 teens per librarian
Mess Factor: Medium

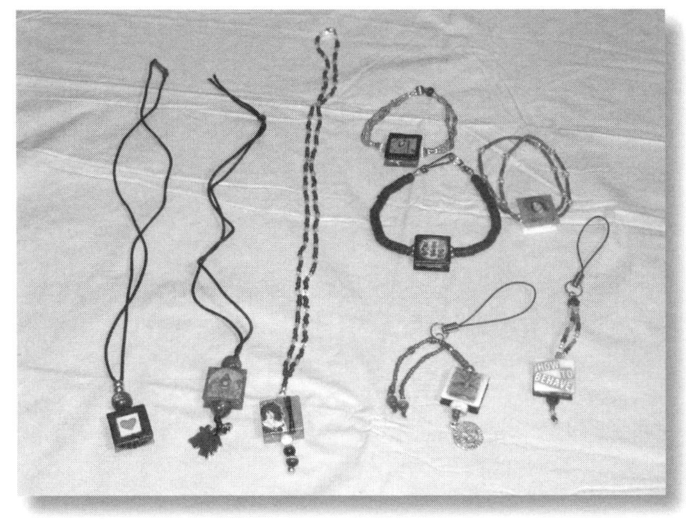

Finished mosaic tile jewelry pieces: necklaces, bracelets, cell-phone charms

THIS PROJECT, ALTHOUGH a little time intensive, is relatively easy, and your teens will be creating a few pieces of wearable art that can showcase their personal styles.

Tailoring this project to various types of programming is as easy as changing the types of paper scrap you provide for your participants. If you're running a manga or graphic novel program, give them some back issues of *Shojo Beat* or *Wizard* magazine. If you're using this as a part of a cultural diversity program, have catalogs and pictures of various cultural icons or scenes at the ready. Animals, flowers, games, sports—the possibilities are endless. You can even make the project more directly book focused by making the tiles look like book covers. You can ask your teens to bring in their own magazines or even color copies of their own photos (make sure these are small enough to fit the tiles).

This project is best done in two sessions. In the first session, the teens will be choosing the pictures and creating the tiles. In the second session, they will string the beads and tiles into finished jewelry. Once the group gets going, you'll find tons of images to adorn these tiles, and it's easy to get quite a stack ready to use. You're bound to have teens who work at different speeds, so plan enough time for each teen to make at least three pieces of jewelry. The best way to do this might be to set up a four-week program, spending the first week making the tiles and the subsequent weeks concentrating on each type of finished piece.

A printable one-page instruction sheet for this program is available on the book's website: www.ala.org/editions/extras/Coleman09713.

Supplies and Tools

beading or jewelry glue
beading needles
containers (small mint tins with lids are perfect)
craft knives and/or small scissors (cuticle scissors work well)
decoupage medium
foam brushes
paint pens (the ones specifically for glass and tile)
pencils
pliers or tweezers
polyurethane varnish (clear)
scissors (regular size)
Styrofoam trays
water in small containers

Materials

assorted beads
jewelry clasps (optional)
jewelry cording
mosaic tiles, 1 inch by 1 inch (you need the ones with grooves along the back)
paper scrap to decoupage (discarded comics, catalogs, children's books—anything with small images)
pin backs
small embellishments (sequins or jewels)
stretchy beading cord

Room Requirements

table (covered with newspaper or drop cloth)
large wastebasket

Prep Work for Session 1

Getting the Project Ready

Do a few test tiles yourself ahead of time, as well as a finished piece of jewelry, to have something to show the group. Review your paper scrap supply and pull out sources that will yield the best results for this project. Resources that work particularly well for this project are comic books, discarded graphic novels, and book or movie catalogs. Anything with images small enough to fit on the tiles will be useful.

If you want to pare this project down to a single session, you can create all the tiles yourself ahead of time and let your teens choose which tiles to string for their jewelry.

Getting the Room Ready

Cutting out the images and decoupaging the tiles are relatively simple processes and shouldn't require special setup. Because the project will extend over two sessions, each participant will need a Styrofoam tray and a small container to hold the cutouts. Each person should also have small scissors, a craft knife, or both. After participants are finished cutting, each person will need a foam brush, water, and decoupage medium. The paper scrap and tiles can be left in the middle of the table so everyone can take what she or he needs.

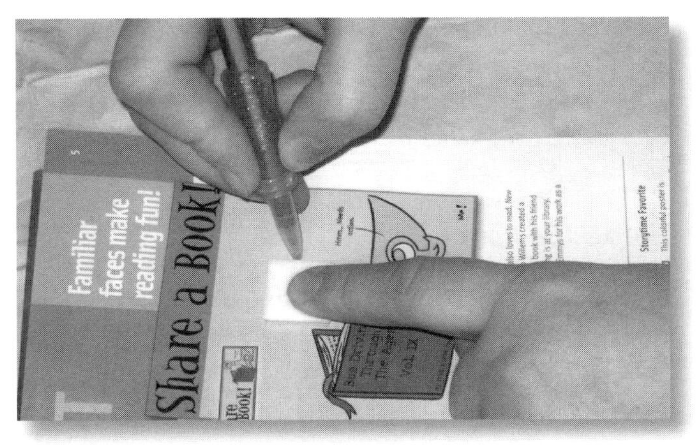

Tracing around a tile to make the image the correct size

Cutting out the image with cuticle scissors

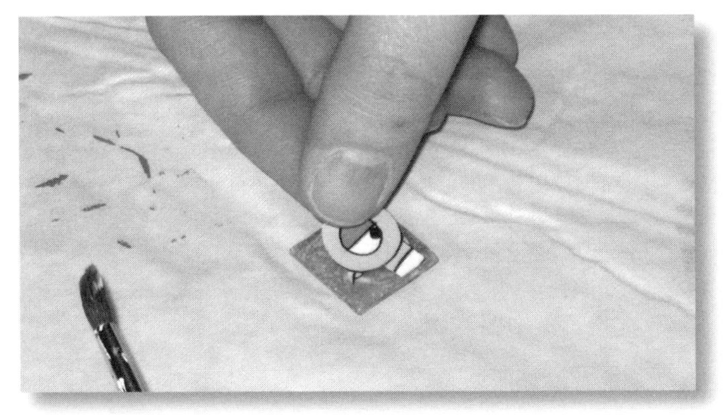

Decoupaging the trimmed image to the tile: Step 1

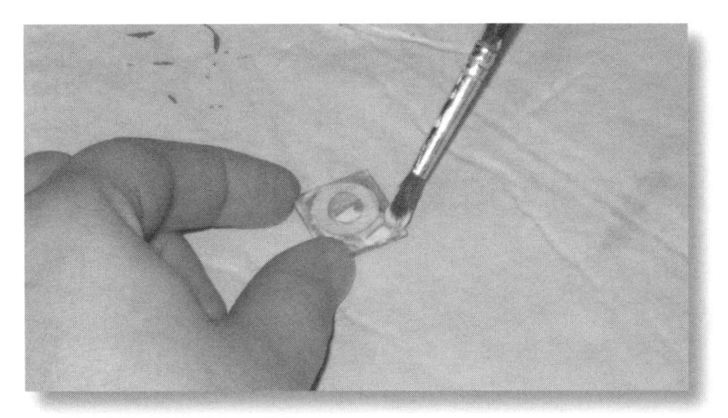

Decoupaging the trimmed image to the tile: Step 2

Directions for Session 1

Step 1: Collecting Images

Leaf through the paper scraps and find an image that you like and that will fit on the tile. Cut around the image. If you need to, use a tile to draw a square pattern and cut along the outline. Put the image aside in your small container. Keep in mind that you can also cut out words to use.

If you want to forgo the paper scrap and design your tile from scratch, use the paint pens and draw directly onto the tiles.

Think of this phase as building a collective pool of cool images for the group to use later.

Step 2: Decoupaging

When you have the supply of images you need, you're ready to start decoupaging. Brush a light coat of decoupage medium onto the tile. Place your image on the tile. The decoupage medium stays wet long enough for you to move the image around if you need to. Once you have the image placed where you want it, brush on another coat of decoupage medium. Put aside to dry.

As you're decoupaging, think about how the tile will be used. The grooves on the back of the tile will need to align for stringing later. For bracelets, the

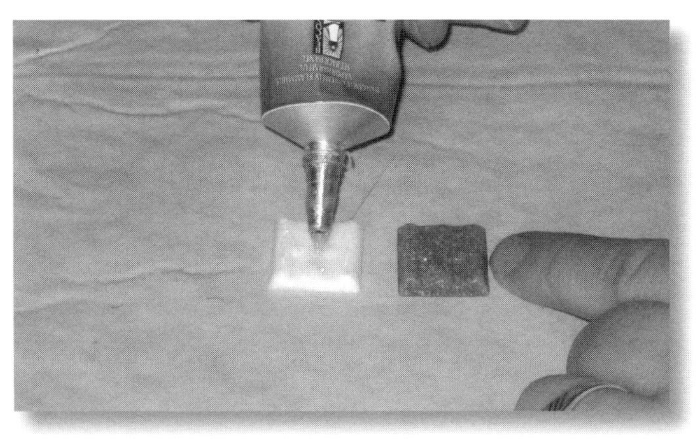

Applying jewelry glue to tiles along the back ridges

grooves should go side to side, whereas for necklaces or complex pins, the grooves should go up and down.

While your first tile is drying, you can make more tiles exactly the same way.

Step 3: Sealing

When all your tiles are decoupaged and dry (drying should take about fifteen to twenty minutes), use a clean brush to add a light coat of polyurethane varnish. Let dry for about twenty to thirty minutes. The polyurethane doesn't need to dry completely, but it should be dry enough to touch without leaving fingerprints.

Step 4: Finishing

When the tiles are dry enough to touch, glue them back-to-back with the grooves running parallel to each other. Try to keep the grooves as clear of glue as possible so you can run cord through later. Tiles can be glued together as pairs, so each side has an image, or back-to-back with blanks.

When all the tiles are glued, leave to dry at least twenty-four hours. This is the end of the first session.

Prep Work for Session 2

Getting the Project Ready

Go through the finished glued tiles and make sure any strings of glue or excess blobs are trimmed off. You can usually do this with a craft knife.

Getting the Room Ready

For each participant, set up a tray of completed tiles, beading or regular needles in a few sizes, and a pair of scissors. Beads, cording, stretchy string, pin backs, and so on can be placed in the center of the table for everyone to take as needed.

Directions for Session 2

You can make several different types of jewelry with your tiles. Each type will have its own special steps, so decide what you want to make first. It's best to complete one piece before starting another.

Planning a bead design for a bracelet

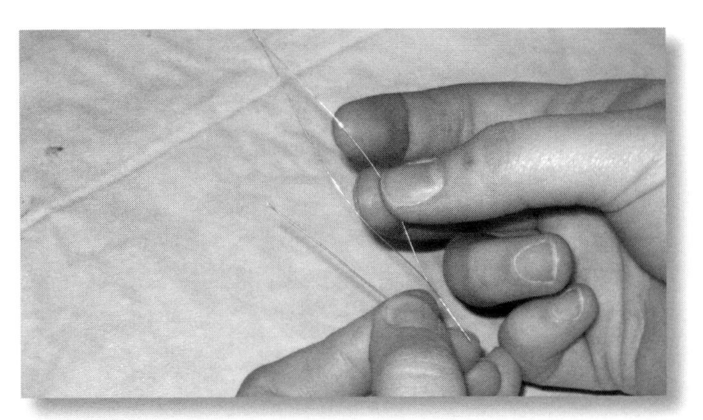

Beading needle with large eye

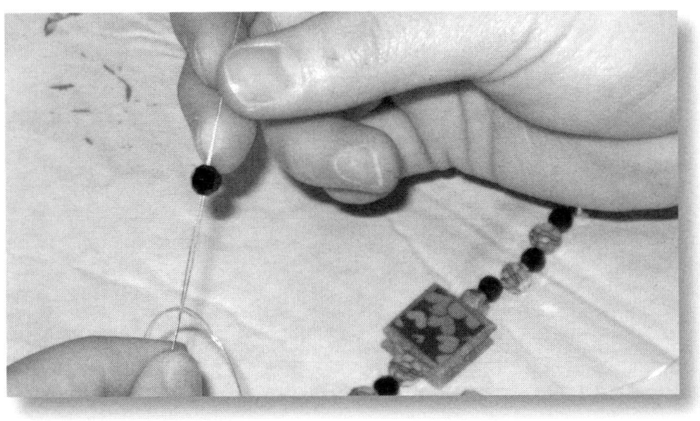

Using a beading needle: Stretchy string is threaded through the large eye, and the beads move easily along the flexible needle onto the string.

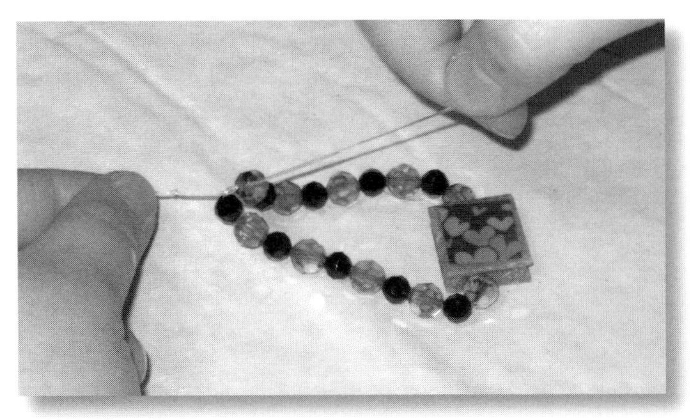

Tying off a bracelet with multiple knots

Bracelets

STEP 1: DESIGNING

Using the stretchy string, measure your wrist. The stretch in the string will allow the bracelet to slip over your hand but fit snugly on your wrist without the stretch. Before cutting, add some extra length to tie a knot to close the bracelet at the end. You'll need at least 3 inches extra. You'll need two strands of stretchy string cut to the same length. When you have the string cut, lay it out flat on your workspace and start laying out your tiles and beads. Because the tiles have two grooves, you'll need two strings to stabilize them, but this also means they work well for double-strand bracelets as well. For a double-strand look, plan your layout accordingly.

Tip: Bracelets look best with one or two tiles per bracelet.

STEP 2: ASSEMBLING

Leaving a 1½-inch tail, tie the two strands together. Choose a beading needle, making sure it fits through the beads you're working with. Thread one or both of the strands through the beading needle, depending on whether you have a single- or double-strand layout. String the beads as your layout dictates. If you're using different-size beads, you may need to change your beading needle as you go.

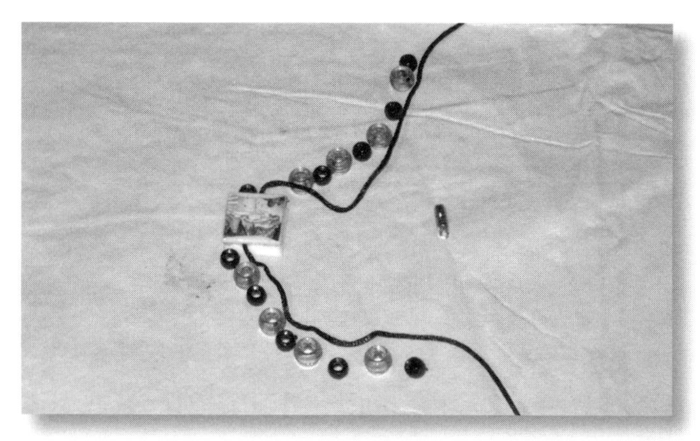

Planning a bead design for a necklace

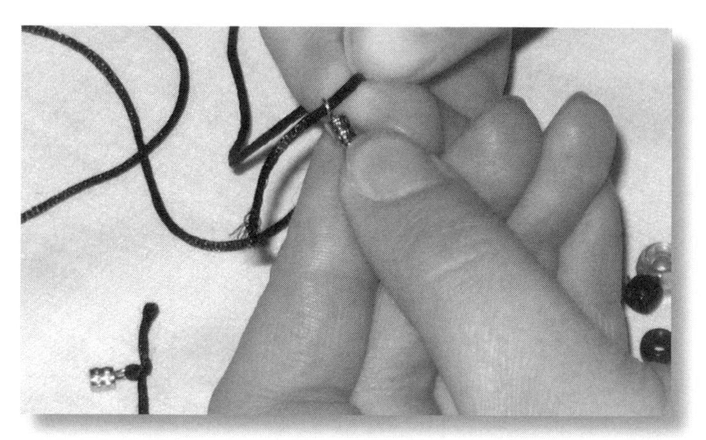

Adding a clasp to the necklace string

Adding a clasp to the necklace string

Planning a bead design for a complex pin

STEP 3: TYING OFF

Once you have your bracelet beaded, double-check the fit around your wrist before tying off. You may find that you need to add or remove a few beads. When the length is correct, tie both strands into a secure knot. The stretchy string can be slippery, so you may need to double your knot. Make sure the beads don't pass the knot. You should have at least 1½ inches of string at the end.

STEP 4: CLOSING AND FINISHING

Tie the tails together twice, making sure to pull the knots tight and secure. You may want to secure the knot with a dab of glue.

STEP 5: EMBELLISHING (OPTIONAL)

To add extra flash or flair to your pieces, glue small sequins or jewels to the faces of the tiles. As you're gluing make sure to use just a small dab of glue to hold the jewel or sequin in place.

Necklaces

STEP 1: DESIGNING

Cut the cord to the desired length, leaving room for knotting or adding a clasp. Once you have your string cut, lay out your tile and/or bead pattern.

STEP 2: ASSEMBLING

If you're planning a fully beaded necklace, knot one end of the cord, leaving a tail long enough to tie the necklace around your neck, or add a clasp later. Choose a beading needle, making sure it fits through the beads you're working with. Thread the cord through the beading needle. If your necklace is a simple pendant design, string the tiles and beads as you have them laid out. Keep in mind that knots in the cord can be quite decorative as well.

STEP 3: TYING OFF

If you have a fully beaded design, tie off the end with a secure knot that's big enough to stop the beads from falling off. Be sure to leave another tail at this end to tie the necklace on, or add a clasp.

STEP 4: CLOSING AND FINISHING

If you're adding a clasp, simply tie the ends of the string to the wire loops on the clasp. These loop attachments may look slightly different depending on the type of clasp you are using, but the string should tie in essentially the same way on most types.

STEP 5: EMBELLISHING (OPTIONAL)

To add extra flash or flair to your pieces, glue small sequins or jewels to the faces of the tiles. Make sure to use just a small dab of glue to hold the jewel or sequin in place.

Pins

STEP 1: DESIGNING

Plan your pin with any beads or tiles you'll want to use. Once you have your layout established, cut the cord that will hold the piece together. The cord will loop through the design in a U shape. Make sure to leave enough extra cord to tie your knots.

STEP 2: ASSEMBLING

For a simple pin of a single tile, glue a pin back to the back of the tile, let dry, and you're done. You can even do this without gluing the tiles back-to-back—a good use for any stray tiles that don't have a partner.

For a dangling pin, knot one end of the cord. Choose a beading needle, making sure it fits through the beads you're working with. Thread the cord through the beading needle. Add your beads and tiles according to your layout. When you get to the top of the design, loop the

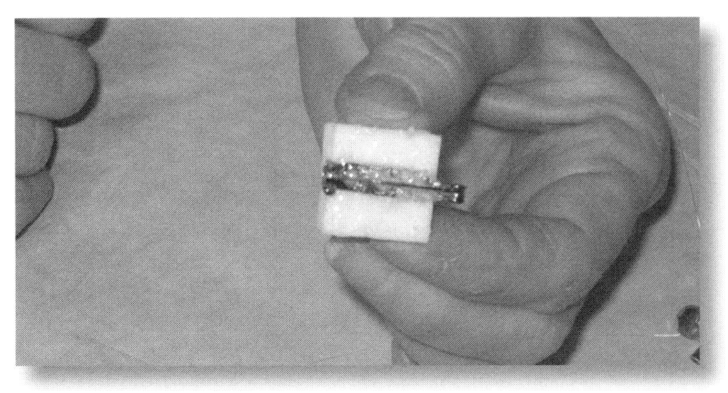

Bar-pin back glued into place on a simple pin

Clutch-pin back glued into place on a simple pin

Tying off a beaded design on a complex pin

Bar-pin back glued into place on a complex pin

cord into a U shape and travel down the other side of your layout. Keep in mind that knots can be decorative as well.

STEP 3: TYING OFF

For a dangling pin, tie off the end to make sure the beads won't slip over. Trim the tails.

STEP 4: FINISHING

Glue a pin back (bar or clutch) to the back of the top tile and let dry.

STEP 5: EMBELLISHING (OPTIONAL)

To add extra flash or flair to your pieces, glue small sequins or jewels to the faces of the tiles. Make sure to use just a small dab of glue to hold the jewel or sequin in place.

Spin-offs

Pushpins, magnets, barrettes or hair ornaments, cell-phone charms, zipper pulls, key chains.

Notes

Woven Paper Baskets

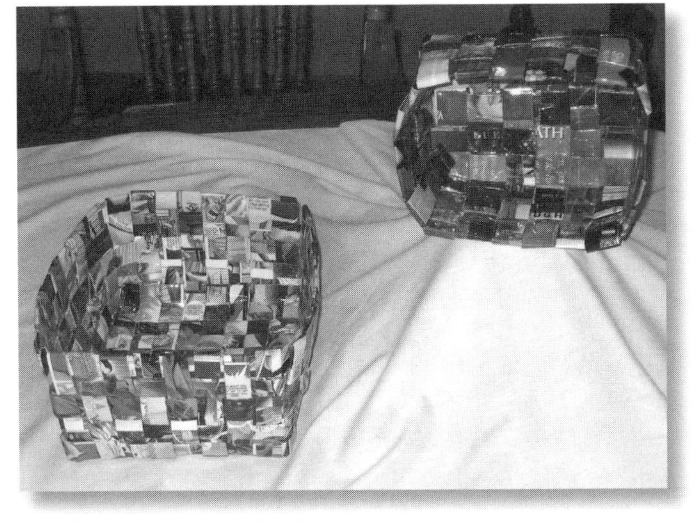

Finished woven paper baskets

Difficulty: Easy
Time: 1–2 hours
Supervision: Light
Group Size: 6–8 teens per librarian
Mess Factor: Low

SIMPLE WEAVING WITH a basic over/under pattern is a straightforward technique that most teens are already familiar with or are able to pick up easily. Weaving with laminated strips of paper allows for some varied and unique results. And did we mention it's fun?

Depending on the kind of paper scrap you make available, you can tailor this craft to almost any type of programming. Using any type of scrap can build the project into a recycling or environmental program. Using seasonally themed pictures or gift wrap can tie it in with holiday programming (e.g., using pictures from gardening magazines for a Celebrate Spring theme). Using pages from graphic novels or comic books as a tie-in for a Get Graphic teen campaign is another fun and colorful way to fit the baskets into your library programming. The project is easy and requires light enough supervision that it can be used as a quick drop-in project or as a rainy-day activity.

The finished baskets are colorful and decorative. Teen groups, pages, or other library staff members can be enlisted to whip some up for parties, open houses, or other events. Or frame the craft as a game by forming teams of three teens each (a folder, a laminator, and a weaver) and have them compete to weave a basket of a certain height.

It's also easy to add variations to the project by changing the width of the paper strips. If the project is a success, encourage teens to look up other weaving techniques that they can try with the strips. Different techniques can produce a variety of different patterns or shapes.

A printable one-page instruction sheet for this program is available on the book's website: www.ala.org/editions/extras/Coleman09713.

Supplies and Tools

burnishing tools (1 for each participant)
masking-tape
packing-tape dispensers
place mats (plastic or vinyl)
scissors (1 for each participant)

Materials

packing tape (thicker gauge, at least 2 inches wide)
paper scrap

Room Requirements

2 tables (covered with vinyl tablecloth)
large wastebasket
several small wastebaskets

Prep Work

Getting the Project Ready

Start by getting your paper scrap ready. If you are using this craft as a part of specific programming and want to reflect that in the paper scrap, this is the time to choose appropriate pieces. Magazines and graphic novels work particularly well for this craft. The paper is a good weight, and the pages are the right size. Plus, you want scrap with full-page images. Lots of bright colors help too. Of course, if you wish, you can use pages of text or monochromatic images. These are design decisions, so have at it and let your creativity soar.

The project itself is pretty easy, but making the strips can eat up time. If you have limited time for your teens to work, tearing the pages out, cutting the pages in half, folding the strips, and laminating with tape can all be done ahead of time.

If the teens are making the strips as well as weaving the baskets, make sure you have enough scissors and tape dispensers to go around. The tape dispensers are especially important—one for every two participants is a good arrangement.

Getting the Room Ready

Have the paper scrap stacks on a side table that's easy to get to but out of the way of the action on the main table. Each participant should have scissors, a burnishing tool or equivalent, and a plastic or vinyl place mat (cheap plastic cutting boards work as well and should be available at the local dollar store).

Have a large wastebasket centrally located for big messes, but place several smaller ones around the table so teens can get rid of tape scraps or strip snafus easily. Cover your table with a vinyl or plastic tablecloth or even a dollar-store shower curtain. This will save your tables from getting tape and adhesive on them and make it easier for participants to reposition tape.

Directions

Step 1: Choosing Your Pages

Leaf through the paper scrap, pulling out pages with images that jump out at you. Keep an eye out for color, texture, and small details. Because the pages are going to be cut in half, then folded, then woven, full images won't be preserved, so you're looking for images that will be interesting in pieces. Keep in mind that it's possible to plan out themes of color or texture. It's fine if you end up with raw edges along the ripped side of the page.

The number of pages you'll need will depend on how narrowly you fold the strips and how big you want your basket. Baskets with large bottoms are not as sturdy as baskets with smaller bottoms and should therefore be shorter. Baskets with small bottoms can go higher with less structural difficulty, but they allow a smaller space to weave as they get taller.

For our example, we are going to use strips that are about ½ inch wide and will make a smallish basket with a bottom of 5 strips by 6 strips. For this basket, we used about 30 strips.

Bad image choice (left) versus good image choice (right)

Step 2: Folding

Fold and crease the page in half lengthwise. Tear or cut along the fold so you end up with two pieces of about equal size.

Taking one of the halves, fold at the edge lengthwise about ½ inch. Crease tightly with your burnishing tool. Fold and crease again and again until you have a ½-inch strip of folded paper. Use your burnishing tool to make sure the folds are as tight as they can be.

Repeat this process with all your pages.

Note: Although we're using ½-inch strips here, you can fold the pages into wider or thinner strips. If you choose wider strips, you may need to use an entire page rather than a half, and your finished basket may be less sturdy.

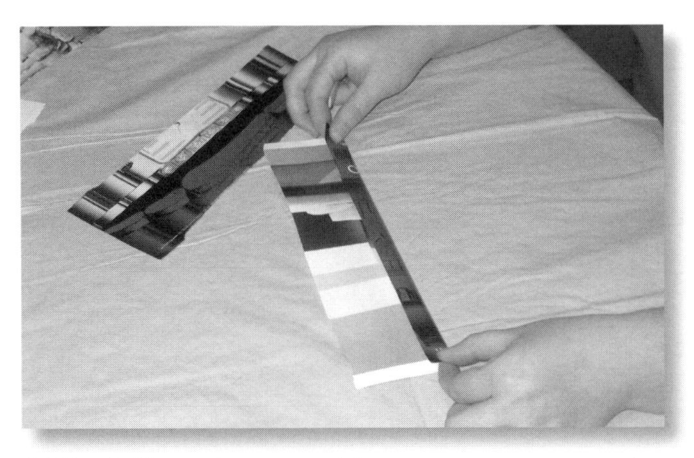

Folding half page into paper strips

Step 3: Laminating with Packing Tape

Laminating the strips with packing tape is easy. Start by laying a strip out in front of you horizontally. It's a good idea to use a vinyl or plastic place mat to tape on. You can easily pick up the tape if you need to move it around or if it sticks to the mat, and you'll be able to move your work around at different angles. If there is a seam on one

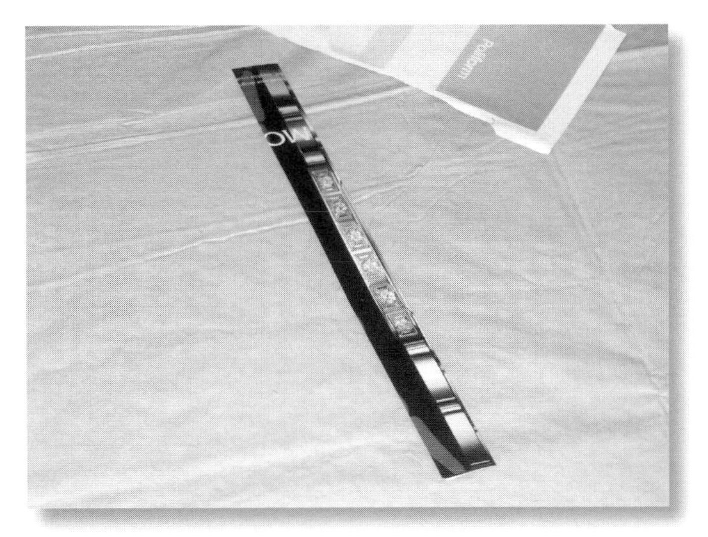

Folded strip

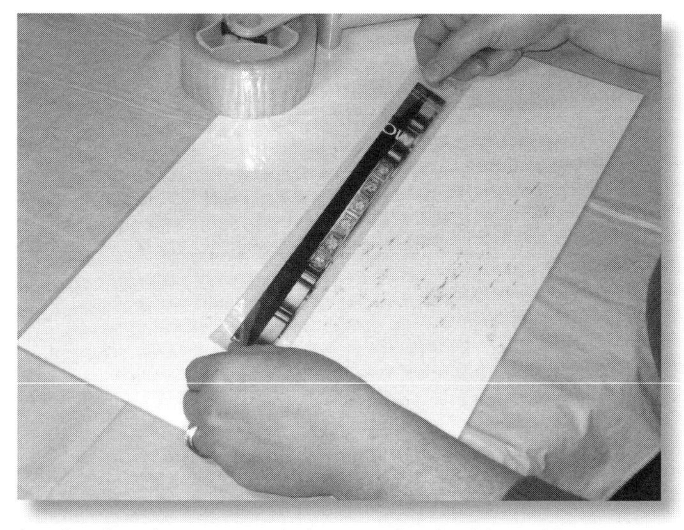

Laminating the paper strip by covering it with packing tape

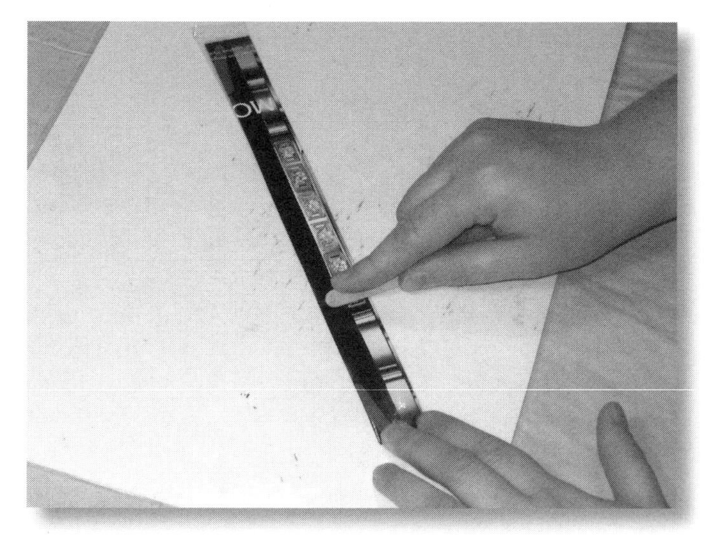

Burnishing the tape down to remove all air bubbles

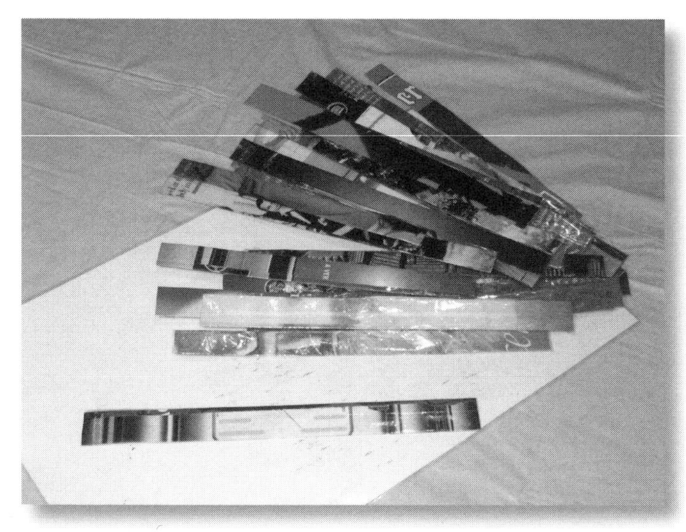

You will need plenty of paper strips to make your basket.

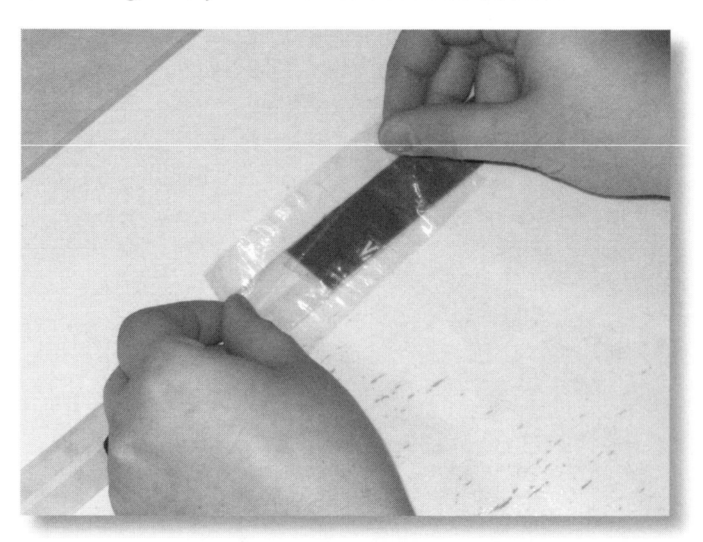

Taping two strips together to create the long strips needed for the basket's bottom and side frames

side of the strip, face that up. Pull a length of tape from the dispenser that is slightly longer than the paper strip (about ¼ inch should do). Holding the tape horizontally by the edges, lay it as straight as you can onto the strip. Press the tape down firmly, then fold it over the sides until the strip is entirely covered in tape. Snip the tape ends closer to the paper. Now use the burnishing tool to flatten out any air bubbles and seal the tape securely.

Repeat this for each of the paper strips.

If you are using wider strips, you may need to use more than one strip of tape. Make sure to overlap the edges of the strips to get full coverage.

Note: If you have a laminating machine at your library, you can use it for this project, but be warned: you'll go through a lot of supplies.

Long strips positioned for weaving and taped to plastic placemat to keep them secured

Weaving the first cross strip at the center of the long strips

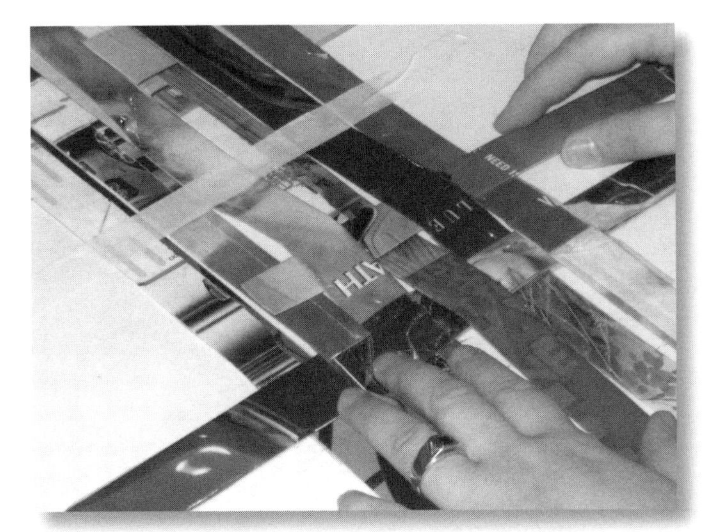

Weaving the second cross strip above the first

Step 4: Weaving

BOTTOM/BASE

Laying strips out next to each other will help you determine how wide your basket will be. When you have the size of your basket in mind, you're ready to lay out your strips and prep them for weaving. To begin, assemble the strips that will form the bottom and frame of your basket. The frame and the bottom need strips that are twice as long as the ones you'll weave the sides with, so tape two strips together for every strip you need. These strips should be about the same length and width, so keep this in mind when you choose which strips to use.

For our example, the bottom is 6 strips by 5 strips, so including doubling their length, we'll need to start with 22 strips.

When you have all your strips taped together, lay 6 out vertically on your vinyl place mat. They should all be lined up evenly from top to bottom, and placed right next to each other edge to edge. Use a strip of masking tape to tape the strips to the place mat along the top ends.

Weave your first strip, over and under, across the center of the vertical strips. (You should be able to easily spot the center at the point where you taped the two strips together.) Once you have the center strip in place and with even tails on either side, complete the bottom by adding the rest of the strips evenly on either side. For ours, we're adding two more strips above the center and two below.

When all the bottom strips are in place, check that the center strip is still in the center. If it isn't, get it back to where it needs to be. Push and adjust the rest of the strips so your weave is tight with no gaps.

When you're satisfied with the weave, use a small piece of tape to secure each corner.

Securing the woven strips with tape

Bending the long strips up from the bottom to form the frame for the side of the basket

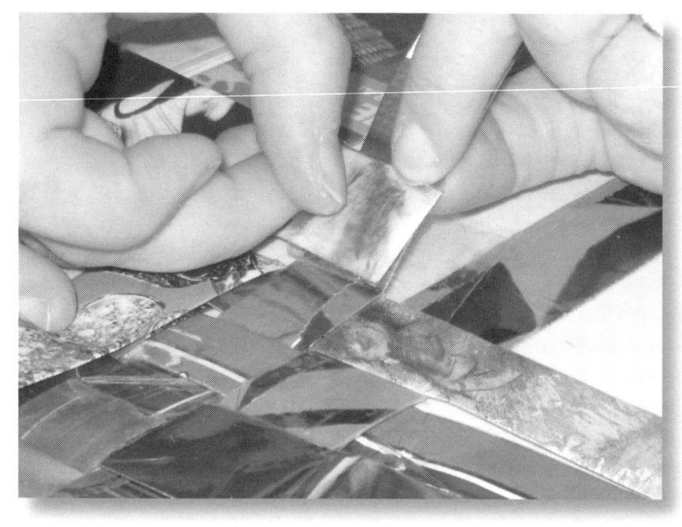

Taping down a strip to anchor it to the frame pieces before beginning to weave

Weaving the paper strip around the corner of the basket

After weaving the strip, taping the end to secure it to the frame of the basket

Adding the next strip

SIDES

With the bottom secured, begin the sides by folding up the tail edges all along the bottom. Crease the folds well, using the burnishing tool if you need to.

These tails are going to be the frame for your sides. When all of them are folded up, take another strip and tuck its end under the middle frame strip on one side at the bottom. Use a small piece of tape to secure it. Weave the strip in through the rest of the side. When you get to the corner, crease the weaving strip so it will turn the corner more smoothly, and then continue around the corner. When you have the strip completely woven through, go back and push it down, making sure the weaving is tight. Then secure it with tape at the corner and at the end. Begin the next strip where the previous one left off and continue with the same technique.

When you have woven all the way around and come back to the beginning of your first strip, tuck the tail for a neater look or clip it away if you have a lot of excess. Weave the subsequent rows in the same way, building your basket to the desired height.

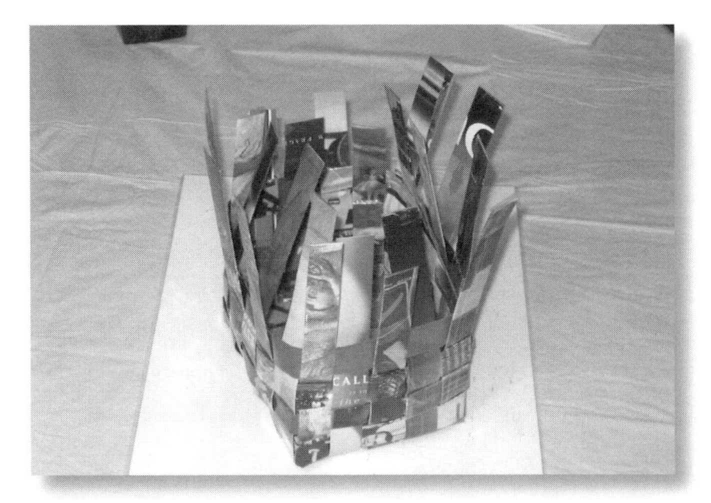

After all the sides are woven in, the basket will have a fringe at the top.

Tucking the ends of the fringe into the weave

FINISHING THE TOP

When you finish the sides, the tails of the frame strips will still be sticking out from the tops. These should be about 2 inches long. With the side strips secured with tape and the weaving tight, you can now secure the top edge. To do this, fold the top tail over the top strip and tuck it under the strip second from the top. Some of the top tails will fold out and some will fold in. You may need to use your burnishing tool to tuck the ends under. If a tail seems loose, use a small piece of tape to secure it.

Once all the tails are tucked in, your basket is finished!

Spin-offs

Mouse pads, place mats, reading journal covers, picture frames.

Adaptations

This project can be scaled down for younger kids by dropping the lamination steps and using regular desk tape to secure the weaving. You may want to have a smaller group as well, if you think the kids may need more help. As is, this project can be a fun parent-child activity or a reading buddy project for teens and younger kids or patrons with developmental disabilities. If you make the strips ahead of time, kids can have fun making temporary shapes with them as well.

Notes

Vinyl Totes

Difficulty: Hard
Time: 2–3 hours
Supervision: Medium
Group Size: 6–8 teens per librarian
Mess Factor: Light–medium

Finished vinyl totes

THESE VINYL TOTES are a bit difficult to construct but well worth the effort. We recommend that you try making one before presenting this project to the group so that you know the basic construction. *Warning*—these totes are addictive! Once you start making them, you will find many pictures that will make beautiful, artistic totes. You will have to make several for yourself and friends.

This project is a great introduction to a book club or summer reading program—participants come away with a very original bag to carry their books! You can also use this project for a photography or art club, a specific book group, a poetry club, and an ethnic or geography study group.

These totes also make wonderful gifts for friends and family.

A printable one-page instruction sheet for this program is available on the book's website: www.ala.org/editions/extras/Coleman09713.

WEB

Supplies and Tools

- binder clips
- burnishing tools or wooden craft sticks
- cardboard (lightweight) or heavy card stock
- containers to sort materials
- embroidery floss and needles
- glue sticks
- hole punches (heavy-duty)
- packing tape (high-quality) with dispenser
- pens or pencils
- rulers
- scissors
- Styrofoam trays
- thimbles

Materials

- buttons, snaps, beads for closures and embellishments
- clear vinyl (available at fabric stores) or a clear vinyl shower curtain

heavy cording
leather or plastic cord or embroidery floss for lacing the panels together
pictures to create the panels; 10 pictures per bag (Look for pictures in recycled calendars; magazines [the heavy, glossy travel or fashion magazines work best]; and garden, nature, animal, or children's picture books that are worn and on the "throw away" list. Book dust jackets, comic book or graphic novel pages, photos, large postcards, posters, or large graphic magazine inserts also work well.)
ribbon and/or strapping for the handles

Room Requirements

2 tables
large wastebasket
several small wastebaskets

Prep Work

Getting the Project Ready

This project has a lot of steps so you will want to organize your materials very well.

Lay out the clear vinyl on a large table or hang it over a door overnight to straighten. Cut the vinyl to square-yard pieces for manageability (no need to be exact).

Gather the pictures that your group can choose from. You can also ask the participants to bring in pictures, photos, or their own original artwork. Using original art and photographs is especially fun if you're using this project with your art or photography groups. If possible, have a sample of this project to show the teens ahead of time so they can think about the pictures and materials they would like to use.

If you want to save time during the work session, cut the vinyl and the pictures to the necessary sizes ahead of time.

Make the hole punch templates. To make a template, measure and cut cardboard ½-inch wide, then measure and mark ½-inch increments for holes (20 holes are good for the length of the totes, and 25 for the bottom). *Note:* The size of your tote will dictate the number of holes needed, but once these templates are made, you can use more or fewer holes as necessary.

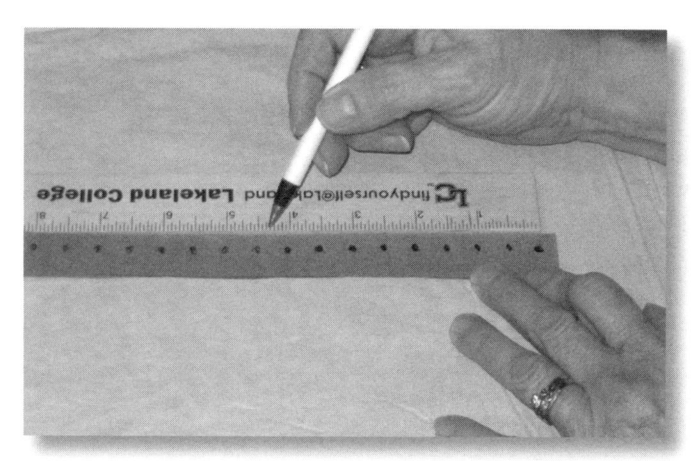

Measuring the markings on the guide for the holes

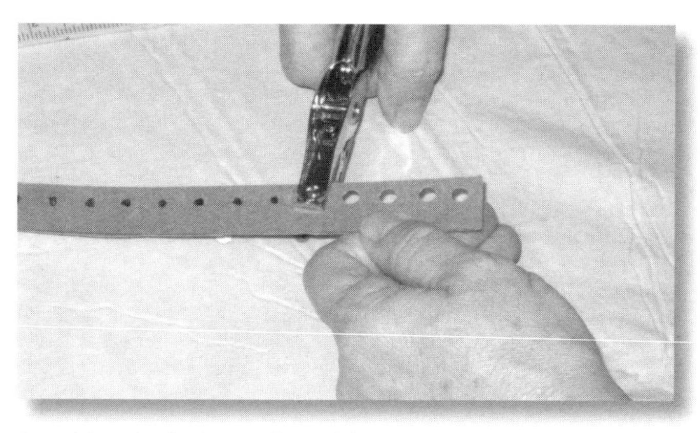

Punching the holes on the guide

Getting the Room Ready

Set up each place with scissors, ruler, glue stick, pen and pencil, hole punch, wooden craft sticks, and instructions. Place cardboard or card stock in the center of the table.

Set up a side table with the pictures (sort the pictures by types and weight, such as calendars, photos, magazines and book jackets, etc.). Place the vinyl pieces in a neat pile. Place the cording, ribbon, and strapping that is to be used for the handles in a container. Place the cording for lacing and the embroidery floss and needles in another container. Place buttons, snaps, and embellishments in a third container. Labeling these containers will be helpful.

Directions

Step 1: Choosing Materials

Read all the instructions first!

Have two or three teens at a time go to the side table to choose their pictures, strap and lacing materials, vinyl, and closures and embellishments and take them back to their places. Each participant will need ten pictures, two for each panel.

Step 2: Laying Out the Design

Choose your largest pictures for the front and back panels of the tote. Your choices will determine the final size of your tote. Trim your pictures as needed to make them neat and even (use your ruler). You should end up with four pieces for the front and back. Choose which pictures you want to be facing out and which to face in. Then put the pictures aside.

Tip: Look at your pictures closely and center them so that the best part or color of the picture shows and is framed well.

Cut your side panels as tall as the front and back panels. Then cut the width of the side panels to, at most, half the size of the front and back panels. It's very important that both of the side panels are the same size, so you may want to cut them at the same time. Again, you will end up with four pieces for your side panels. As with the front and back, choose which images should be facing inside and which should be facing out. Line them up and set aside.

Cut the bottom panels. These should be as long as the front and back panels and as wide as the sides. You will end up with two pieces for the bottom. Again, choose which image should be facing up into the inside of the tote and which will face down outside.

Take a quick measurement to make sure all your panels will match up.

Step 3: Forming Panels

Glue the pictures for each piece of each panel together, back-to-back. If you are using pictures on lightweight paper, you will want to reinforce them with thin cardboard. Measure and cut the cardboard to the same size as the pictures. Glue the pictures onto the cardboard.

Make sure each image is facing in the right direction!

Lining up pictures for the front panel

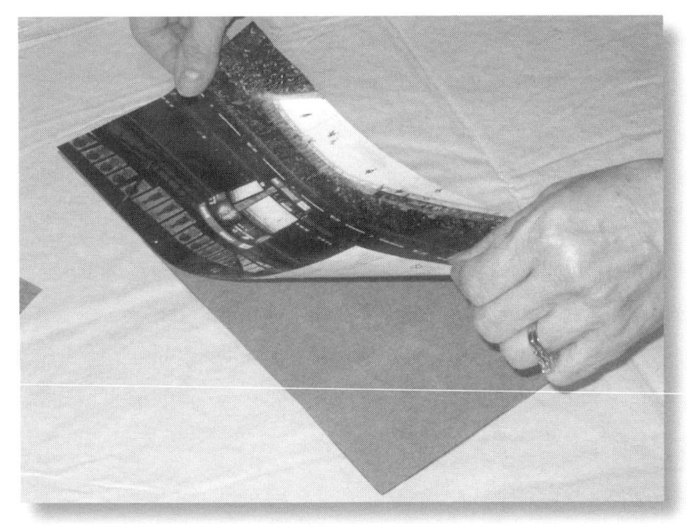

Gluing the bottom image to sturdy cardboard backing

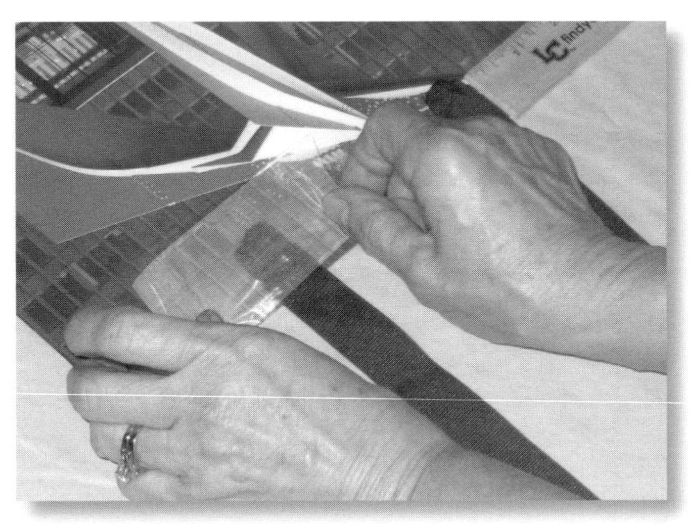

Taping the handles to the inside of the front panel

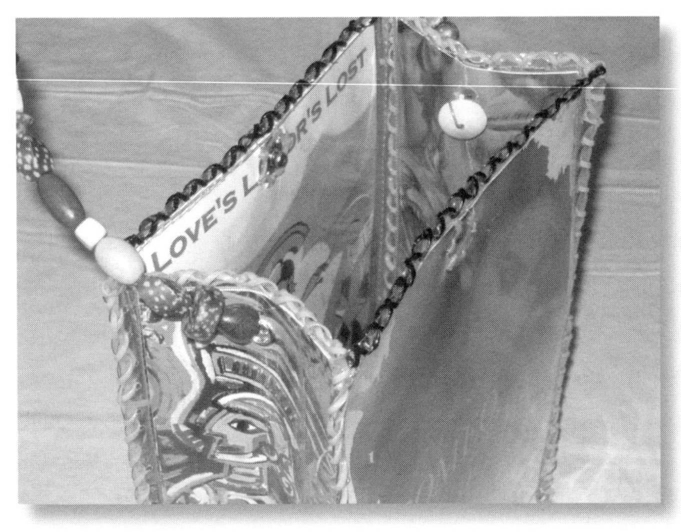

Handle variation: Beaded wire anchored through grommets in the side panels

Step 4: Planning Your Handles

Decide if you want long handles for a shoulder bag or shorter handles for a shopping or purse-type bag. Using the cord, ribbon, or other strap supplies, cut your handles 2 inches longer than the desired length.

You can attach the handles in one of three ways:

1. Arrange the handles centered on the *inside* of the front and back panels allowing for a 2-inch overlap. Glue into place on the inside of the panel and tape over with packing tape.
2. For a single strap or handle, arrange the handle centered on each side panel, glue into place, then tape over with the packing tape.
3. Sew or grommet the handles to the front and back panels or to the side panels. (These handles would be attached to the tote after it is completed.)

Step 5: Cutting the Vinyl

Once the teens have their panels prepared, give them the clear vinyl pieces.

Fold or layer the vinyl. Carefully trace around the edges of the picture panels onto the vinyl and cut on that line. You will need two pieces of vinyl for each panel.

Sandwich the panels between the two pieces of vinyl and lay out to make sure everything fits well.

Step 6: Taping

For this step you will need to clear your space.

Start with the front panel. Line up the picture panels and the two vinyl pieces and clip into place with binder clips. Keep the edges as even as possible.

Pull out a strip of packing tape long enough to cover the top edge of the panel. Lay the tape on the table, sticky side up. Place the panel on top of the tape so that an equal amount of tape will be on each side. Carefully fold the tape over the panel edge and smooth it into place. Watch for wrinkles or air bubbles and smooth the tape down firmly.

Continue taping all edges of the panel, moving the binder clips as needed to hold the pieces together. Check the taped panel and smooth out any wrinkles with your finger or a wooden craft stick.

Tape all the edges on all the panels in this way.

Lay out all the taped panels on the table as they will go together.

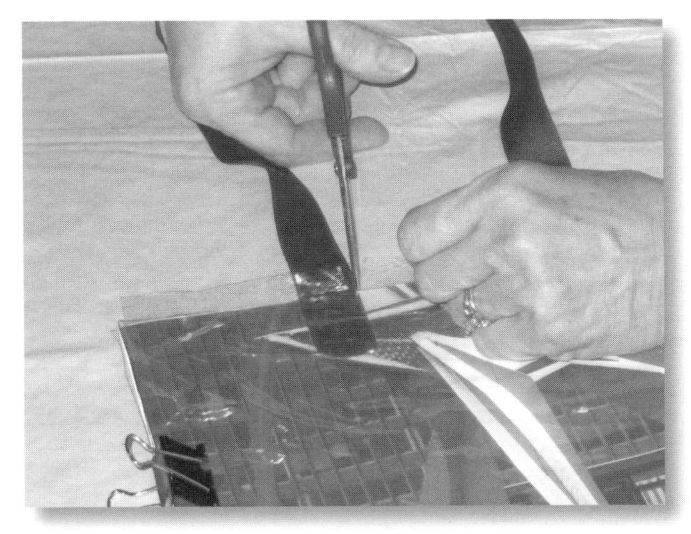

Trimming the excess tape from around the handle

Burnishing the taped side down

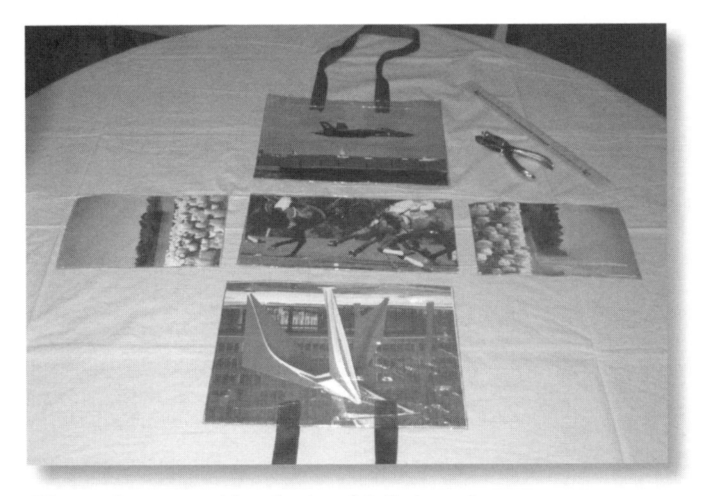

All panels, covered by vinyl and fully taped, laid out in the correct positions for lacing

The hole guide clipped into place along the edge of the front panel

All panels after the holes have been punched

Lacing the bottom and side together, and adding the front panel

Securing the corner lacing and the front panel

Detail of finished laced corner

Step 7: Punching Holes

Using the premade hole punch guides, determine how many holes you will need to lace your tote together. Line up the hole punch guide on the long side of one of your side panels and use two binder clips to hold it in place.

Get your hand muscles ready and punch each hole through all the layers of the panel. Do the same with the other side, bottom, and front and back panels until complete.

Once you finish, you should have holes on each edge of all your panels, *except* the top edges of the front, back, and side panels. You can do the top edges if you'd like to add lacing for embellishment.

Step 8: Lacing

Tied clasp

Line up one of the side panels with the bottom panel along the short edge. Make sure that the bottom panel is indeed lining up with the bottom of your side panel. Thread cord through all the holes on this edge. Tie a knot at the end of the cord (leaving a 2-inch tail) to secure the cord in place without pulling it through behind you.

Once that bottom side edge is laced, bring the back panel into place. Again line up the holes, being careful that your images are facing in the same direction. Carry the lacing over from the bottom/side seam into the first hole on the bottom edge of the back panel. Then with your next loop, lace the bottom edge of the back to the side edge of the bottom. When you get to the end of the back/bottom seam, tie off your lacing securely and clip the cord. Leave a tail to make sure things don't come unraveled. You'll go back and glue the knot at the end.

Snap clasp

Next, lace together the back and the other side panel (top to bottom). Again tie a knot at the beginning of your lacing to make sure things stay in place. As you come to the bottom of the seam, lace through the last hole of the back side *and* the first hole of the bottom panel. Continue lacing along the bottom, and then up the other side of the side panel, bringing the front into place.

Next, going into the finish, lace the bottom of the front panel to the long side of the bottom panel, then continue up, lacing the front to the opposite side.

As you go, be mindful of the length of your cord. You can tie a section off as you go and pick up with a new strand, but you should try not to do so in the middle of a panel edge.

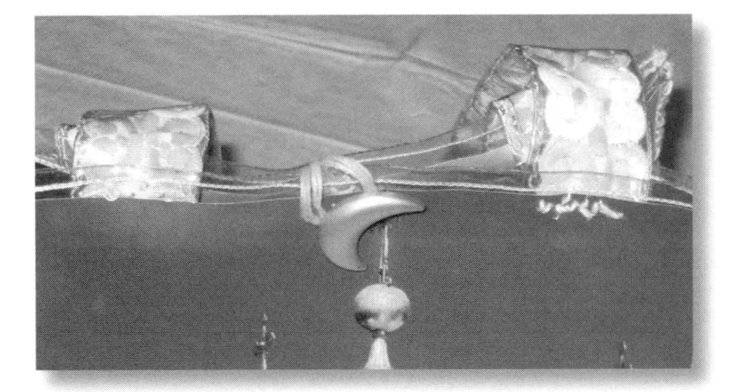

Button clasp

Step 9: Attaching Closures

If you want to put a closure on your tote, here are three ways to do this:

1. Punch a hole in the center of both the back and front panels. Tie lengths of cording to each hole, and use as a tie closure.
2. Sew a large snap to the center of the front and back panels.
3. Punch a hole at the top center of the back panel. Thread a sturdy piece of yarn or string through the hole so both ends are on the inside of the bag, with a loop of yarn on the outside. Tie the ends in a large knot so the yarn won't slip through the hole (it may take more than one knot). This creates the loop portion of your closure. On the opposite panel, sew a large button on the outside of the bag. The loop of yarn should slide securely over the button for the closure.

Spin-offs

Baskets or boxes, wallets, change purses, personalized gift bags.

Adaptations

You can use this project as is for an adult crafting group or even for a parent-child project. Just make sure all your supplies and materials are organized and easy to search through.

Notes

T-shirt Reconstruction

Difficulty: Easy–hard
Time: Variable
Supervision: Light–medium
Group Size: 6–8 teens per librarian
Mess Factor: Medium messy

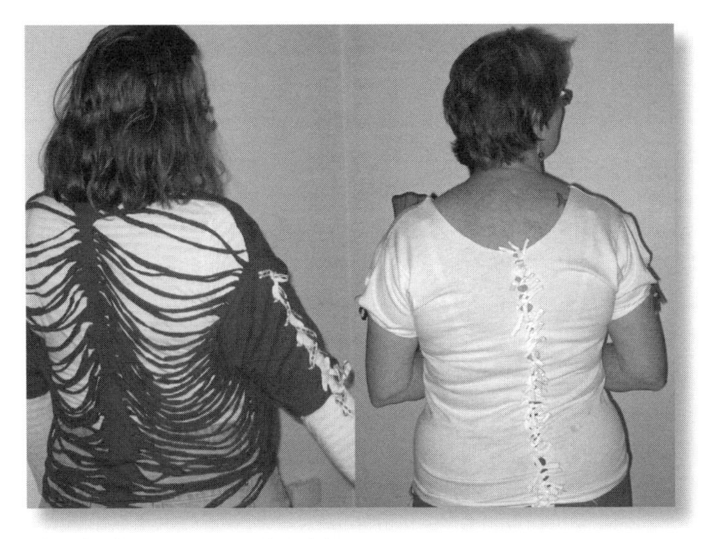

Finished reconstructed T-shirts

T-SHIRT RECONSTRUCTION HAS become a cornerstone of the crafting community, spawning discussion groups and communities across the Internet. The project allows nearly infinite possibilities of design, construction, and technique, and it can be tailored to almost any difficulty level, time frame, and supplies on hand. As a result, it is the perfect craft to bring into the library. Even if you decide not to use this project with a group, it will give you something creative to do with that drawerful of old conference and concert tees.

Although the instructions we present here are more for individual use, T-shirt reconstruction can be adapted for your teen group. Plan a fashion show for your teens to present their designs or have your own version of *Project Runway* complete with judges. Any way you frame it, this project is a great way for teens to express their creativity and unique personalities. As an added bonus they get a fabulous piece of wearable art to show off their creativity with pride.

Whole books are dedicated to this project, so we will just present some basic techniques that you can use singly or in combinations to create tons of unique shirts. Keep in mind that T-shirt reconstruction is a down-and-dirty, ever in flux, truly DIY craft. This means there are many different ways to do any particular technique, but it also means that there is absolutely no *right way* or *wrong way* to do things either. Let yourself be creative. Treat it like sculpture and let the T-shirt tell you what it wants to be. Once you begin to see how a shirt—or any piece of clothing, for that matter—is really put together, ideas on how to change it will come to you.

The basic supplies you'll need are included in our main list at the end of the book, and we'll warn you if you need something special for a specific technique.

A printable one-page instruction sheet for this program is available on the book's website: www.ala.org/editions/extras/Coleman09713.

Supplies and Tools

- basic sewing supplies
- measuring tape
- seam ripper
- sewing machine (technically optional, but will make your life much easier)
- straight edge or ruler (1 for each participant)
- tailor's chalk (1 for each participant)

Materials

- embellishments
- fabric and other scrap clothing to use for spare parts
- T-shirts (good to have long- and short-sleeve varieties available)

Room Requirements (for a group)

- 3 tables (you may need an extra table if you're working with a large group to make sure everyone has enough space to work)
- large wastebasket
- several small wastebaskets
- large mirror or access to a room with a large mirror

Prep Work

Getting the Project Ready

It's good to have some spare parts already cut out and on hand for teens to choose from. Sleeves cut from other shirts, wildly patterned fabric, pockets cut away from jeans or dress shirts—all are useful pieces to have available. Take the time to put some finished sample shirts together to inspire the teens. If your group is large, you may want to restrict the project to only a few different techniques.

Don't forget to ask teens to bring T-shirts from home. Each participant should come with at least three shirts.

Getting the Room Ready

Done in a group, this project can get loud, so setting up a separate room may be best. Participants should feel free to collaborate or exchange ideas. You could even have the teens pair off to work together.

Participants will also need easy access to a mirror to check fit or progress or to judge results. If you don't have a large mirror in the room, you may want to let them go in groups to a nearby washroom.

Set your fabric, spare parts, and embellishments on a side table. The main table(s) should be kept clear so participants have room to lay out their work to cut or pin. If you have a sewing machine, set it up on a separate side table and make sure it is threaded. If you have the luxury of two machines, thread one with light thread and the other with dark thread.

Directions

The first step for all these techniques is to *try your shirt on*. Look carefully at your shirt and think about what you like about it and what you don't like about it. Check the fit—does it need to be tighter or looser? Is there a logo or design on the front that you want to preserve? Is it too long? Too short? Decide how you want to reconstruct your shirt before you cut or sew.

Look through the directions for each technique to get a sense of what you want to do.

Technique 1: Lacing (No Sew!)

Extra materials/supplies/tools: grommet pliers and grommets; ribbon, cording, or some other lacing material.

Lacing will add a more fitted and feminine look to a T-shirt and give you some options on how to accessorize a look. Lace with delicate ribbon for a softer, bohemian look, or lace with leather cording for a sassier, punky look.

PLANNING

To begin, you need to decide a few things:

Where will you put your lacing? The location of your lacing will directly affect the fit of your shirt. If you want your shirt to cinch in and be really structured but you have a lot of extra shirt, you should do two lacings, one on either side. For easy adjustability, you should have one lacing up the back of the shirt. If you're feeling funky and you want to really play with the look, you can plan your lacing to go across the front of your shirt. Or you could add lacing to the sleeves, or one in the front and one in the back. It's a versatile technique that can be a nice decorative feature.

How far apart will you put your grommets down the line? And how far apart will your rows of grommets be? The spacing of the grommets will affect how tightly and how evenly you will be able to lace. Wide-set grommets work well if your lacing is mainly for decoration. Close-set lacing will give you more control over the cinch and fit of your shirt. For the spacing from grommet to grommet down the line, we recommend no more than 2½ inches and no less than ½ inch. For the placement across the line, no more than 6 inches and not less than 3 inches. Of course, if the lacing is purely decorative, you can deviate from these measurements to your heart's content.

How long should your lacing be? Lacing from collar to bottom hem can be striking, but it is not usually a practical solution for fit.

MEASURING AND MARKING

For this example we are going to do one lacing up the back of our shirt from the bottom hem to midback with close-set grommets. We are going to have our grommets 1 inch apart down the line and our rows separated by 6 inches.

Lay the shirt out flat on the table, face down. You'll need to draw guidelines with tailor's chalk to mark the placement of the grommets. Start by finding the centerline for the grommets. To do so, measure across the back of the shirt at about midsleeve seam height and divide by two. Using the straight edge, draw a line at that point all the way from the collar to the bottom hem.

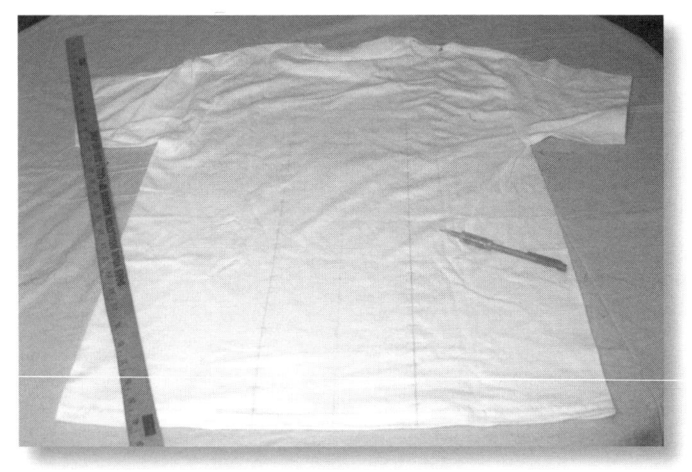

Lacing: Back of T-shirt with measurements for grommets marked

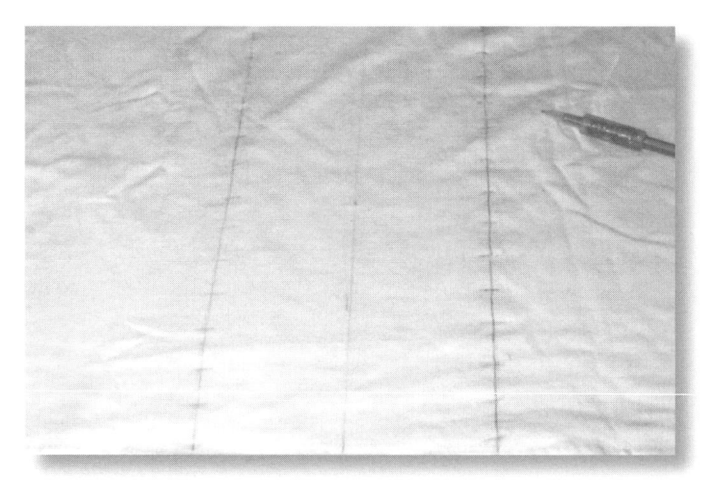

Lacing: Back of T-shirt with marks for grommets

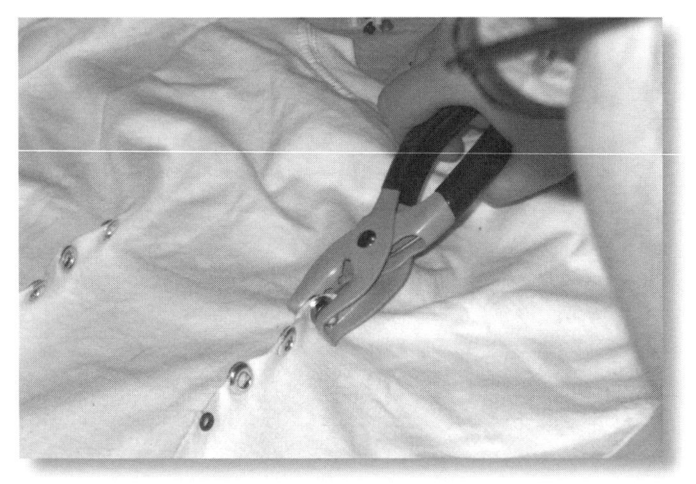

Lacing: Adding grommets with grommet-setting pliers

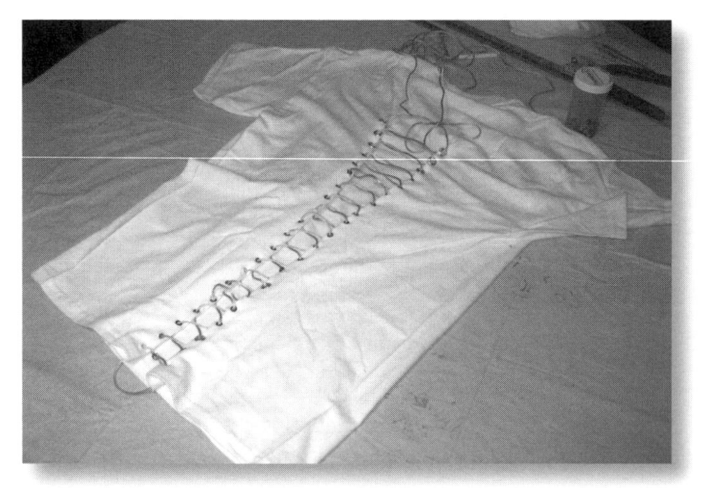

Lacing: Laced with cord, from bottom to top.

Divide the row separation measurement (6 inches) by two. Measure and mark this distance (3 inches) from the centerline on either side. Repeat this at the top, middle, and bottom of your centerline to have as exact a guide as possible. Draw your guidelines on either side, and you should have a pattern on your shirt that looks like the picture in the upper-left corner.

Now you need to mark exactly where the grommets will go. Line up your straight edge across the shirt at roughly the height of the shoulder blade. Make a small mark across each of the two guidelines. Then measure down from that mark in 1-inch increments, marking the spots for all the grommets in each row. Now our shirt looks like the picture in the upper-right corner.

Now, pinch up the fabric at each of these points and use the grommet pliers to insert grommets.

FINISHING

When all the grommets are in place, use a damp cloth to wipe away your chalk marks. If that doesn't work you may need to rinse the shirt in water or wash it and let it dry before lacing.

After the marks are cleaned away, lace (like a shoe) and you are done.

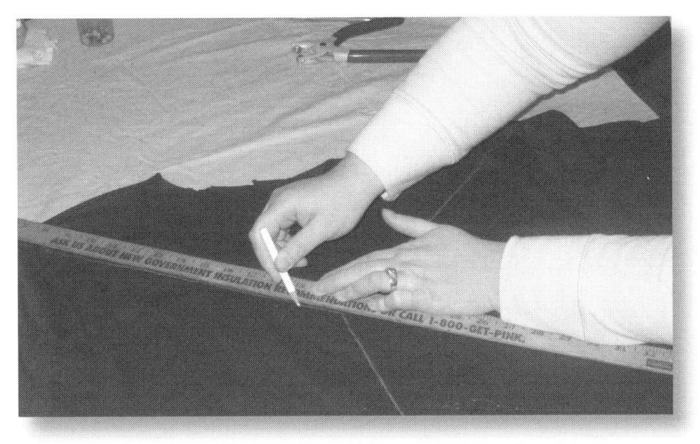

Snip-tying: Measuring and marking a pattern for the cuts

Snip-tying: Cutting on Y marks

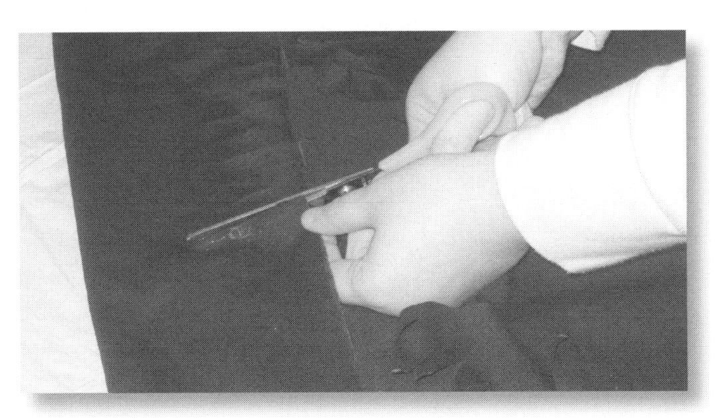

Snip-tying: Snipping the fringe into the cut edges of the shirt

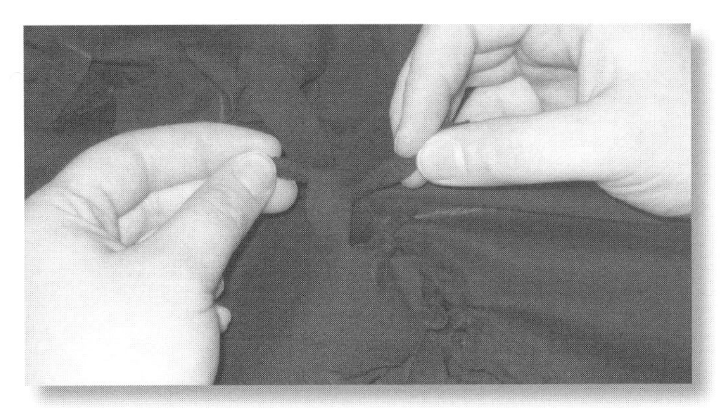

Snip-tying: Tying the fringe to create the snip-tied effect

Technique 2: Snip-Tying (No Sew!)

Snip-tying is a really useful, quick way to alter a T-shirt on the fly. It can be quite decorative and adds texture as well as design. It does subtly alter the fit of a shirt, so keep that in mind when snipping your tighter tees.

Our example is going to work a Y design into the back of our shirt, but this technique can work almost anywhere.

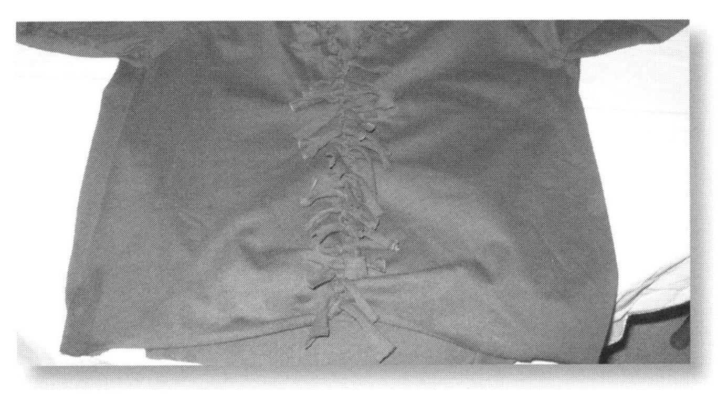

Snip-tying: Finished shirt

MEASURING AND CUTTING

Start by laying the shirt out on the table, face down. Measure across to find the center and mark with chalk. Using a straight edge, draw in the lines of the design.

Now we have our Y in place and it's time to cut. Because we have a design that would come away from the shirt if we cut completely, we're going to start with cutting only the middle line and one of the arms of our Y.

Next, along both raw sides of the cut, snip into the fabric so you end up with a fringe along both edges. The depth of these cuts affects the fit of your shirt. You need at least 1½ inches to tie them off well, but if your shirt is really big, feel free to make the cuts longer. Here we used about 2 inches. There is no need to be precise.

Razoring: Pattern design drawn onto shirt

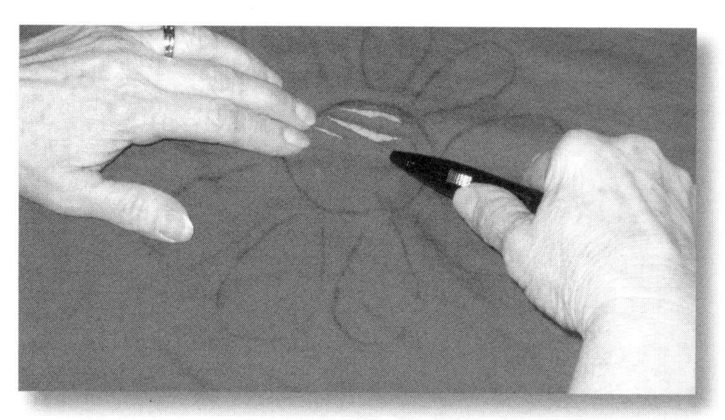

Razoring—Method 1: Using a sharp utility knife to cut slits into the design area

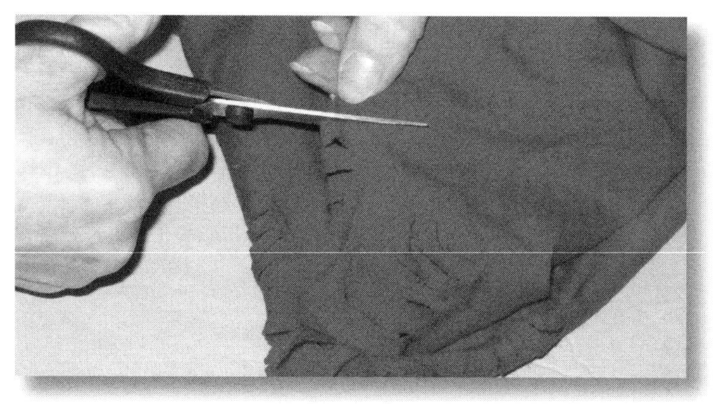

Razoring—Method 2: Using a sharp pair of small scissors to cut slits into the design.

Razoring: Finished razored design

FINISHING

When the entire fringe is cut, go back and tie the two edges together with the fringe. Work your way all the way up until the entire seam is tied.

For our example we repeated the process on the other arm of the Y and then we were done.

Technique 3: Razoring (No Sew!)

Extra materials/supplies/tools: sharp razor or very sharp small scissors; thick cardboard.

Razoring involves adding cuts close together to add pattern and texture to a T-shirt that can then be layered over another shirt. You can use razoring to make simple shapes (circles, squares, hearts, etc.) or to go all the way across the back or front of the shirt. Depending on the shapes you use, this can be a very guy-friendly reconstruction.

DESIGNING

Start by laying the shirt out flat on the table with the part to be razored facing up. If you're using a razor, put the thick cardboard inside the shirt so you don't cut through the other side of the shirt. Use tailor's chalk to sketch out your design. Remember, if you make a mistake with the chalk, you can just rub it away with a damp rag.

Franken-shirting: Cutting through the stack of shirts

CUTTING

Once you're satisfied with the pattern, you're ready to cut. For our example we traced out a simple flower design.

If you're using the razor, *be very careful.* Make sure you hold the razor safely and pay close attention as you work. Stretch the T-shirt tightly against the cardboard, and cut across your design. Start at the top of the design and move down, cutting lines inside the design as you go. Space your cuts about ¼ to ½ inch apart. *Do not cut around the edges of the design.*

If you are doing this technique with a group, use scissors rather than a razor. Cutting with scissors will be easier and will give you more control, although the cut edges will look less raw than the razor cuts.

Once the design is filled in with cuts, you're done.

Technique 4: Franken-shirting

Extra materials/supplies/tools: at least 2 T-shirts; spare parts from other pieces of clothing; straight pins.

Franken-shirting is the art of cutting apart different shirts and reassembling them into a new design. This can be as basic as swapping the sleeves or collar from one shirt to another or as complex as creating a patchwork T-shirt from several shirts. You can create some unique fashions, especially if you bring in other types of shirts. For example, you can add the cuffs, collar, and button-up pieces of a dress shirt to a long-sleeve tee and end up with a classy look. This is another guy-friendly technique.

For our example we're going to work on a patchwork tee made from four shirts of about the same size. As an added bonus we'll reassemble each of the shirts and end up with four versions of our patchwork shirt.

PLANNING AND DESIGNING

This technique takes a closer look at deconstruction and planning. You may want to try a few rough sketches of your ideas so you know how to cut and where to sew to get what you want. Also, take time to look at how each piece

Franken-shirting: Laying out cut pieces to plan a design

Franken-shirting: Finished Franken-shirt

you're using is constructed and plan how you want to take it apart. Some pieces may work better if you take them off with the seam ripper rather than cutting. Pay extra attention to collars and sleeves.

CUTTING AND ASSEMBLING

Once you have your design firmly in mind, turn your shirts inside out and lay them out to be cut. If you're just cutting and replacing selected parts (sleeves, collars, pockets, etc.), you can remove them from each piece individually.

For our example we're stacking the shirts to make sure we cut pieces roughly the same size and shape. For greater precision, we marked where we plan to cut on the top shirt. Carefully cut the pieces out and pin the layers together. Try to leave the pieces generally in the places they will go.

Once you have all your cuts made, choose which to use and reassemble, pinning the pieces together. Pin everything together to make sure your pieces fit correctly. Once you're sure everything will go back together, remove enough pins so you're dealing with three or four large pieces, each with two or three seams to sew. This will make the project more manageable at the sewing machine.

Sew the seams together, assembling the pieces into a whole shirt.

Notes

Book Pillows

Finished book pillows

Difficulty: Medium–hard
Time: 2–4 hours
Supervision: Medium–high
Group Size: 2–3 teens, depending upon sewing ability and machine availability
Mess Factor: Medium messy

BOOK PILLOWS MAKE excellent gifts as well as nice additions to teens' pillow collections. They feature straps to hold the book open as you're reading or keep your place if you doze off. There's also a handy pocket for a bookmark, book light, or tissues for those tearjerkers on the shelf. The pillows make you want to snuggle up with your favorite book as soon as you finish sewing them. They would be a great item for Friends sales. They are especially good as gifts for kids and teens because they encourage reading and can be bundled together with a book and accessories.

The book pillows are a simple pattern to fit a twin-size pillow. Participants can choose fabrics that coordinate with a particular décor or that remind them of their favorite book or favorite space to read. Some good choices for fabrics are flannel, soft cotton, denim, fleece, or fancy home-decorating fabrics. You can usually find inexpensive fabric in the remnants bin at fabric stores or discount stores. This is also a good project for recycling clothes, curtains, or other fabric participants might have on hand.

A printable one-page instruction sheet for this program is available on the book's website: www.ala.org/editions/extras/Coleman09713.

Supplies and Tools

- heavy paper or poster board cut into pattern template (4 pieces, 1 set for each participant):
  - front/back: 24-by-18-inch rectangle
  - top: 5½-by-24-inch rectangle
  - pocket: 6½-by-4½-inch rectangle
  - straps: 4-by-19½-inch strips
- iron and ironing board
- needles
- pencils
- scissors
- sewing machine
- yardstick

Materials

embellishments
fabric (about 1 yard total for each participant)
threads
twin-size pillow (1 for each participant)

Prep Work

Getting the Project Ready

Draw the template patterns on large heavy paper or poster board. Cut out the following pattern pieces:

one 24-by-18-inch rectangle
one 4-by-19½-inch rectangle
one 6½-by-4½-inch rectangle
one 5½-by-24-inch rectangle

Directions

Step 1: Designing

This is the time to think about the design and theme of the pillow. Participants may want to draw a simple sketch or just have an idea in mind. Teens can take their inspiration from their favorite things or, if they are making the pillow for a friend, choose a theme to fit her or his personality and likes.

Flowers and gardening themes, animals, superheroes, cartoon characters—all can be worked into these pillows. So many types of fabrics and patterns are available that it will be easy to make book pillows for everyone on the teens' gift lists. Just remind participants that they will want to make each pillow fun and inviting.

Teens can also take inspiration from a favorite fabric they would like to reuse. Denim from a worn-out pair of jeans or skirt, cotton from a soft, lacy top, velvet or silk from a much-loved dress—all would make excellent material for pockets, tops, or straps. Tablecloths, curtains, or even soft towels could be used for the front and back of the pillow. A pillow made entirely from a fancy beach towel would be a great summer reading gift for a favorite beach bum.

Step 2: Preparing the Fabric

Wash, dry, and iron the fabric as needed. Lay out the fabric on a large cutting area and pin the pattern in place. If you're using poster board, carefully trace the pattern onto the fabric.

Cut out the following pieces:

two 24-by-18-inch rectangles for the front and back of the pillow (use your main fabric)
two 4-by-19½-inch rectangles for the straps

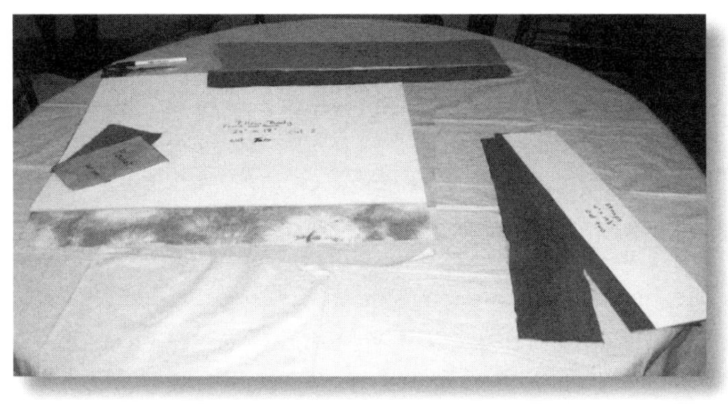

Book pillow patterns, with cutout fabric pieces

Pressing fabric pieces

Pressing fabric pieces

Pieces laid out and pinned

one 6½-by-4½-inch rectangle for the pocket
one 5½-by-24-inch rectangle for the top

Use coordinating or recycled fabrics for the smaller pieces to enhance your theme or design.

Step 3: Pressing

Press the fabric for the straps by folding ¼ inch in on each side of the fabric. Press well so that it stays in place, then fold this in half and press again (pin if needed to keep it in place). Press out the pocket and fold down about ¼ inch for the top hem. Fold ⅛ inch around the pocket's outer edges and press well (pin if needed to keep in place). Press the top piece, making a ¼-inch hem at the bottom. Press well (pin if needed). Press the pillow front and back.

Step 4: Sewing

Set up the sewing machine and thread with matching or coordinating thread.

Sew the straps at the folded edges. You can use a simple straight stitch or a decorative stitch depending on your fabric and the look you want.

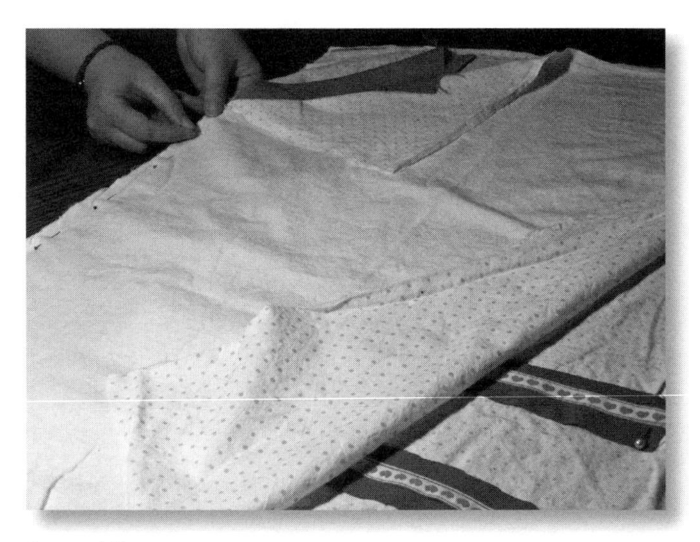

Assembling

Sew the pocket's top hem. If you want to add a decorative trim at the top, this is the time to do it. You could use binding tape or lace ribbon. Sew around the pocket edges. You may want to add other small embellishments such as fabric appliqués or decorative stitching to the pocket to enhance your theme.

Lay out the front of the pillow on the table and place the pocket on the right side about 1½ inches from the bottom and 5½ inches from the right side. Line up the pocket as straight as possible and pin into place. Sew the pocket in place.

Lay out the front of the pillow again and place the straps on the left side. Place the first strap 3¼ inches from the side, and place the next strap 3½ inches from the first strap. (*Note:* You want the straps to be a bit loose so that a book can slide in.) Check for alignment and adjust if necessary. Pin in place at the top and bottom, but don't sew them down. The straps will get sewn when you sew the back and front together.

Place the top piece right side down onto the front piece; place the back piece right side down onto this and pin together. Again, this piece will get sewn into place when the front and back are sewn together.

Sew these pieces together at the top, the right side, and the bottom of the pillow.

Stuff with the twin-size pillow. This will be a tight fit so you will need to wiggle the pillow in, straightening as you go. If you're not careful to keep the pillow straight as you stuff, your pocket or straps can go out of alignment.

Hand sew the left side of the pillow with a tight running stitch.

Done!! Snuggle up with a good book! If your pillow is a gift, add a bookmark or book light to the pocket.

Adaptations

This project can be used for a reading buddy activity or adapted for patrons with developmental disabilities by using pillowcases and attaching the straps and pocket and embellishing as desired. For straps, direct teens to use nonfraying material like fleece or T-shirt jersey or use ribbon or cording. For the pockets, they can use salvaged jeans or shirt pockets. These should all be easy to hand sew with a little direction or glued with fabric glue. Once the straps and pocket are sewn or glued on, insert the pillow and sew or glue the open pillowcase end closed.

Notes

Supplies, Tools, and Project Materials

Supplies and Tools List

beading needles (see glossary)
binder clips
box cutter
brads
burnishing tool (see glossary)
carbon paper
cardboard (see glossary)
card stock
containers (various sizes and shapes)
craft knives
craft sticks (wooden)
cutting boards (wood or plastic)
decoupage medium
dowels
embroidery floss
embroidery needles
fine line permanent markers
finishing nails
glue:
- beading/jewelry glue
- fabric glue
- glue stick
- hot glue
- white glue

glue gun
grommet pliers (see glossary)
grommets
hammer
hand sewing supplies (see glossary)
hole punches (heavy duty)
heavy paper
ink pads
iron
ironing board
makeup sponges
markers
measuring tape
mirror (full-length if possible)
nail polish remover
needles (assorted sewing, curved sewing, embroidery, large-eye)
newspaper
paintbrushes (bristle, foam)
paint pens (the ones specifically for glass and tile)
paint:
- acrylic paint
- craft paint

paper cups
paper cutter (optional)
paper plates
paper scrap (see glossary)
paper towels
parchment paper
pens and pencils for marking
phone books
place mats (plastic or vinyl)
pliers
polyurethane varnish (clear)
poster board
rubber stamps (letter stamps come in handy)
rulers
sandpaper
scissors (large, small, scrapbooking)
scrapbooking punches
seam ripper
sewing machine (optional, but it will make your life much easier)
sponges (small)
stencil brushes and paint
stencils
straight edge
straight pins
tailor's chalk
tape (masking tape, packing tape in various sizes; see glossary)
tape dispenser
thimble
thread
tissue
towels
trays (Styrofoam, plastic; see glossary)
tweezers
twine
vegetable peeler
wastebaskets (large, small)
waxed paper
yardstick

Project Materials List

beads (assorted sizes and colors)
binding rings
bookmarks (blank, premade)
brads
buttons

card and paper stock
cording:
- beading cord (stretchy)
- heavy cord
- jewelry cord
- leather cord
- plastic cord

cork
craft sand (various colors)
craft sticks
crayons
dowels
embellishments (see glossary)
embroidery floss
fabric
fabric scrap (see glossary)
felt
found objects
glitter
grommets
jewelry clasps
magnets (see glossary)
marbles (craft, floral)
mosaic tiles (1 inch by 1 inch; you need the ones with grooves along the back—see glossary)
note cards (blank)
paint: glass paint
paper (wallpaper, wrapping paper, origami paper)
paper scrap (see glossary)
pillow (twin-size)
pin backs (straight and clutch)
polyurethane (clear)
pressed flowers (see how-to in Pressed Flower Note Cards)
razor
ribbon
rubber bands (the best are the small, "no-tangle" hair bands)
scrapbooking vellum pages
snaps (large and small)
tile:
- ceramic wall tiles, white or very light colored (4 inches by 4 inches)
- floor tiles, white or very light colored (12 inches by 12 inches)

T-shirts (long- and short-sleeve)
twine
vellum quotations
vinyl (clear; available at fabric stores or use clear vinyl shower curtain)

Glossary

Techniques

We use several techniques repeatedly in projects throughout the book. Although they are described in the project instructions, here are more distinct definitions or details on how to do them.

BURNISH. To rub with a tool that is specially made for smoothing and polishing. We use this technique in laminating some of our paper projects.

DECOUPAGE. To decorate with cutouts of paper, fabric, or other flat material over which polyurethane is applied. This is a sure-fire technique that anyone can do.

Hand Sewing

BLANKET STITCH. A blanket stitch is a variation on a whipstitch. You start with a whip, then bring your needle through your thread loop and pull tightly. Your stitches can be farther apart. Use this stitch for decorative outside seams. It also works well for topstitching.

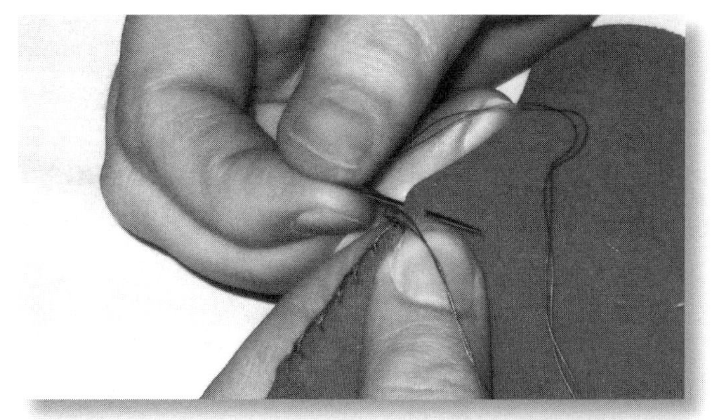

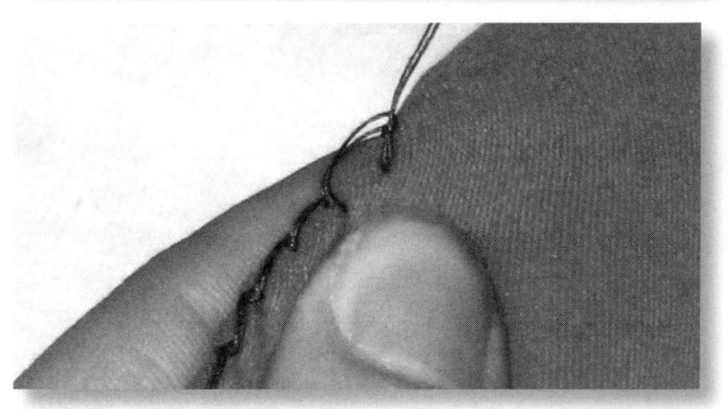

The blanket stitch

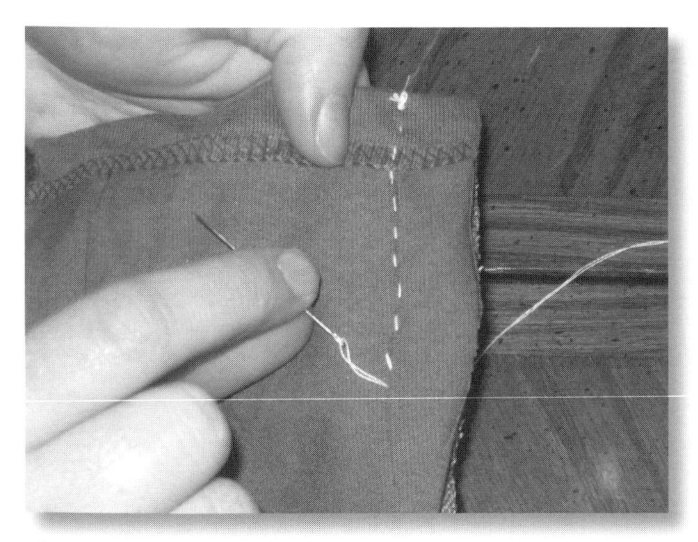

The running stitch

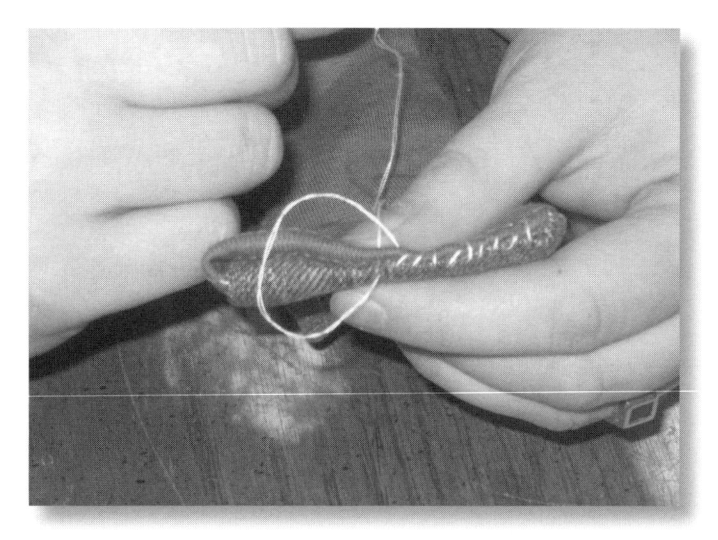

The whipstitch

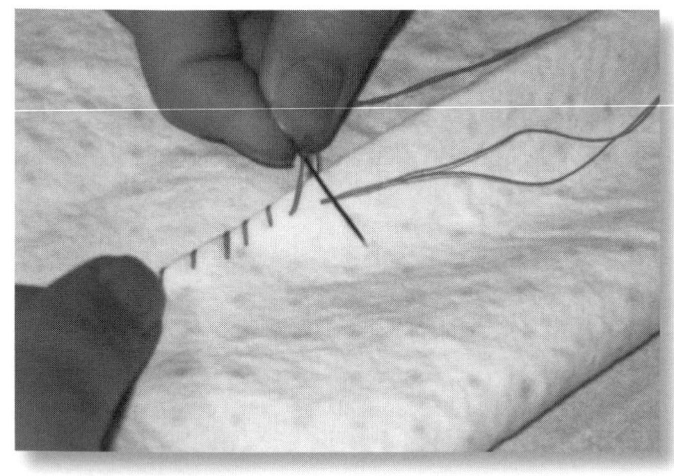

Start/end knot technique

RUNNING STITCH. A running stitch is a basic in-and-out stitch. It's mostly used for inside seams that will not be seen once the fabric is turned inside out, so precise alignment is not critical.

WHIPSTITCH. A whipstitch is a basic stitch that goes over the edge of the seam with the needle always coming up through the fabric in the same direction. It is mostly used for outside seams or decorative touches.

START/END KNOT. Pull the thread through the fabric, leaving a tail. Sew another stitch, this time bringing your needle through the thread loop. Pull tightly, holding the tail as you do. This creates a knot that will anchor your seam.

Tools and Materials

ADHESIVES. Hot-glue guns and glue sticks can be used for these projects. However, hot glue, though a quick solution, is not always permanent. Sometimes other glues are a better and more permanent choice. It's also a good idea to have options on hand if you can. When choosing fabric glue, read the label and make sure it is permanent and washable. Bead/jewelry glue is a quick-set glue and adheres to many surfaces, but it can be messy so make sure to cover the work area. Participants may want to wear disposable plastic gloves.

BEADING NEEDLE. A beading needle is a flexible piece of thin wire with a sharp point and a large eye that will fit through most beads. They are available at most craft supply stores in the beading section.

BURNISHING TOOL. A burnishing tool is a slim, hard plastic stick with a slightly wider curved head. You can improvise a burnishing tool by using a craft stick. In a pinch, your fingernail will work.

CARDBOARD. Several of the projects here call for cardboard in various weights. It's always good to have a supply on hand. Heavier weights from boxes are always useful. If you run across cardboard with interesting textures like egg-carton or corrugated, be sure to add it to your stash.

EMBELLISHMENTS. Embellishments are easily one of the most important materials to have in good supply. Looked at properly, anything can be used as an embellishment. Here are just a few examples of things you should hoard:

beads
computer or other electronic circuit boards
costume jewelry
game or puzzle pieces (collect them from games that are already missing pieces)
key chains
recycled ribbons, yarn, twine (these are easy to find during the holidays)
sequins
small mirrors (you can recycle the mirrors from makeup cases and purses)
small toys
watches and clocks

FABRIC SCRAP. You can find fabric scrap all around—your own closet, garage sales, resale shops, and donations. Some things to look for:

clothing (keep an eye out for leather and suede especially; recycling a leather skirt from a thrift shop is much cheaper than buying leather from a fabric shop)
curtains
fabric remnants
neckties
quilting squares
recycled denims (jeans, shirts, skirts, etc.; denim is one of the easiest fabrics to get and is also very easy to work with)
table or bed linens

GROMMET PLIERS AND GROMMETS. Grommet pliers are special pliers that you can use to punch holes for and install grommets. They are available at most sewing, craft, or art supply stores. The instructions on how to use them are on the packaging, so be sure to keep the package or photocopy the instructions to keep with the pliers. Grommets come in different colors and sizes and should be available in the same aisle.

HAND SEWING SUPPLIES. For any sewing project you should have some basic hand sewing supplies for each participant. The following are recommended:

embroidery floss (assorted colors)
measuring tape
needle threaders
needles (assorted)
pincushions
safety pins
seam rippers
straight pins
tailor's chalk or something to mark fabric with
thimbles
threads (black and white and several basic colors)

MAGNETS. For the magnet projects, use the small, very strong circle magnets available at larger craft supply stores (or on the Internet). Do not use the self-adhesive strip magnet tape. It's not strong enough to support the crafts in most cases.

MOSAIC TILES. For the Mosaic Tile Jewelry project, it's important to use tiles that have grooves on the back deep enough to accommodate the thread or cord for the jewelry. Large craft supply stores have these, but you may need to poke around on the Internet if you can't find them locally.

PACKING TAPE. We use packing tape several times in these projects as an easy seam closer (Vinyl Totes) and as a laminating material (Pressed Flower Note Cards and Woven Paper Baskets). We cannot stress enough how important it is to use good-quality tape in the right width. If you're going to splurge on anything, do it on this item. You want a thicker gauge tape about 2½ to 3 inches wide. Stay away from the cheap, thin packing tape; it will only stress you out. Be sure to have a good tape dispenser on hand as well.

PAPER SCRAP. This is another resource with almost endless uses. Decoupage anything and everything, and use pictures for jewelry, magnets, or paper baskets. Some ideas to get you started:

- book jackets
- books (discarded or damaged travel books, art books, graphic novels, children's books—especially those with bold, artsy pictures)
- calendars
- catalogs
- comics
- greeting cards or postcards (especially those with a vintage or graphic look)
- magazines
- maps
- posters

TABLE COVERING. Although you can use newspaper in a pinch, it's not particularly practical because it can get messy as you work. We recommend using cheap plastic tablecloths from the dollar store or recycling heavy-duty vinyl tablecloths you or your patrons may have on hand.

TRAYS (STYROFOAM OR PLASTIC). Trays are very helpful for keeping the teens organized as they work. Trays make cleanup a little easier as well. You can use Styrofoam trays (recycled from a cafeteria or purchased at a restaurant supply store); plastic cafeteria trays (you may find these at schools, hospital tag sales, garage sales, or discount stores); or clean, recycled Styrofoam food trays (you can save these from your own supply and/or ask for donations).

Books

Blakeney, Faith, Justina Blakeney, Anka Livakovic, and Ellen Schultz. *99 Ways to Cut, Sew, Trim, and Tie Your T-shirt into Something Special.* Potter Craft, 2006.

The Complete Photo Guide to Sewing. Singer Sewing Reference Library. Creative Publishing, 1999.

Easy Beading. Better Homes and Gardens, 2004.

Maresh, Janice Saunders. *Sewing for Dummies.* For Dummies, 2004.

Nicolay, Megan. *Generation T: 108 Ways to Transform a T-shirt.* Workman, 2006.

Websites

Antimony and Lace (www.gothfashion.info)—Check the Projects tab for a list of clothing reconstruction projects that are fun for the gothic-ly inclined. Great for the budding fashionistas.

Craftster (www.craftster.org)—A valuable resource for ideas with a great forum for showing off finished projects and sharing tutorials. This site also has regular contests and swaps. A great way to get into the cool crafting community, no matter what kinds of crafts you do.

Daydreaming on Paper (www.daydreamingonpaper.com)—A fabulous website on journaling with writing prompts and ideas on what to do with blank books.

DIY Network (www.DIYnetwork.com)—DIY and its sister station HGTV now have tons of crafter-friendly shows on the air. This site has projects for the crafty as well as more advanced projects.

Get Crafty (www.getcrafty.com)—More forums to share ideas, tutorials, and finished projects.

LiveJournal (www.livejournal.com)—LiveJournal is huge with tons of communities that change on almost a daily basis, but it's worthwhile to do a search under Interests for "crafts," "crafting," or "crafter" to find communities that allow for showing off projects and swapping ideas.

Stencil Revolution (www.stencilrevolution.com)—Great tutorials on how to make your own stencils with various techniques, tips on materials, and a place to show off projects.

BOCA RATON PUBLIC LIBRARY, FLORIDA
3 3656 0509288 3